Unholy Popes

Originally published in 2006 by The O'Brien Press Ltd. as
Holy Smoke: True Papal Stories That Will Amaze and Amuse

Text © 2006, 2010 by Bob Curran

This 2010 edition published by Fall River Press.

Fall River Press
122 Fifth Avenue
New York, NY 10011

ISBN: 978-1-4351-1593-4

Printed and bound in the United States of America

1 3 5 7 9 10 8 6 4 2

The information in this book has been drawn from many sources, and is
assumed to be accurate. Although every effort has been made to verify
the information, the publishers cannot guarantee its perfect accuracy.

Unholy Popes

OUTRAGEOUS BUT TRUE
STORIES OF PAPAL MISBEHAVIOR

BOB CURRAN

FALL RIVER PRESS

CONTENTS

INTRODUCTION

For almost two thousand years, the office of the Roman pontiff—the supreme head of the apostolic tradition of the Roman Catholic Church in the West—has continued to fascinate both Catholics and non-Catholics alike. Few other religious world leaders command such world-wide respect or occupy such an important place in the spirtual and moral lives of their followers. This is no simple cleric, lama, or imam. ✦ Lama: an Eastern holy teacher (usually in Tibet), Imam: an Islamic holy teacher. ✦ The pontiff traces both his succession and authority directly back to the foremost of the apostles, Peter (hence the title "Petrine Ministry"), who sat at the feet of Jesus and received the office that Christ Himself had established. This spiritual inauguration, of course, gives the position considerable depth and gravitas.

> ## ✂ PAPAL PARTICULARS ✂
>
> **Age of youngest pope when elected:** eighteen (John XII)
>
> **Age of oldest pope when elected:** eighty (Adrian I)
>
> **Longest reign: thirty-two years**
>
> **Shortest reign: one day**
>
> **Total number of popes: 265**
>
> **Total number of popes named John:** twenty-three (along with two John Paul's)
>
> **Pope's license plate: SCV 1 Stato della Città del Vaticano (Vatican City State)**

✝ ✝ ✝

"I also say to you that you are Peter, and upon this rock I will build My church; and the gates of Hades will not overpower it. I will give you the keys of the kingdom of heaven; and whatever you bind on earth shall have been bound in heaven, and whatever you loose on earth shall have been loosed in heaven."

—Matthew 16:18–19 (New American Standard Bible)

✝ ✝ ✝

The official title for the pontiff is "Bishop of Rome," and in this respect he is a humble clergyman. But, of course, he is no mere priest. He is the Vicar of Christ, widely known as the pope—a name derived from the Italian word *papa*, meaning "father," making him, in effect, the father of his church. Every bishop in the West used the term "pope" up until the eleventh century, while in the East, the Byzantine Church used it only to refer to the lowliest priest; it was also a special (though seldom used) title for the bishop of Alexandria. In 1073, however, Pope Gregory VII forbade its use for any other cleric except the Bishop of Rome.

✝ ✝ ✝

ALL NAMES LEAD TO ROME:

- ✦ **Vicar of Christ**
- ✦ **Roman pontiff**
- ✦ **The Pope**
- ✦ **Holy Father**
- ✦ **Papa**
- ✦ **Bishop of Rome**
- ✦ **Successor of the Chief of the Apostles**
- ✦ **Vicar of Peter**
- ✦ **Supreme Pontiff of the Universal Church**
- ✦ **Patriarch of the West**
- ✦ **Primate of Italy**
- ✦ **Archbishop and Metropolitan of the Roman Provinces**
- ✦ **Sovereign of the Vatican City State**
- ✦ **Servant of the Servants of God**

✝ ✝ ✝

The pope's impressive list of titles suggests a cleric of intense moral rectitude and unimpeachable uprightness. But has this been the case? Have popes through the ages fulfilled the lofty expectations that such a great and sanctified office demands? Sadly, the answer is "no."

Although the office itself is sacred, it has been occupied by mortal men with mortal concerns. And although by its very nature the papacy should transcend temporal affairs, it was (and to some extent still is) involved in political and worldly matters.

Thus, numerous occupants of the papal chair have been rogues, pirates, drunkards, debauched men, sex fiends, and criminals. There have even been popes who were not altogether Christian, and one is rumored to have been a woman, which is expressly forbidden by papal rules. Some pontiffs headed Roman crime waves; some started and prolonged wars; some lived extravagant lives; some granted position and power to their illegitimate offspring, making them Princes of the Church; some turned the Holy See ✦ Holy See: the jurisdiction of the pope; the lands in which his authority is paramount. ✦ into a wholly temporal business (which, since the papacy also owned land, it already partly was); and some were much more interested in pleasures of the flesh than matters of the spirit. At least one pope turned the Lateran Palace into a thriving brothel with wealthy Romans paying the Vatican for admission. Some popes were mentally unstable, if not unquestionably mad, while others may not have existed at all—and one pope is thought to have been dead for his entire reign!

There were, of course, unquestionably sincere and holy popes who did much good for the Church. But it is perhaps the deviant pontiffs that interest us most. The incongruity of the sacred office and the shenanigans that occurred within the Vatican's cloistered walls may serve to remind us that

beneath all the grandeur and pomp, the pope is still a human being with all his (or, perhaps in one instance, *her)* failings and idiosyncrasies.

EX-CON POPE

Callistus I (217–222)

Callistus is regarded as the first Christian martyr after St. Peter and his name appears in the oldest martyrology of the Roman Church, the *Depositio Martyrum*, compiled around 354. However, it is highly questionable as to whether he was in fact a martyr. ✦ Martyrology: a catalog of martyrs, usually compiled by the Church. ✦ Historians have pointed to the fact that there were no persecutions during his reign and have suggested that his mythologized "martyrdom" was part of a skilled PR campaign by his followers to get him canonized as a saint—and they were successful.

✝ ✝ ✝

Most information about Callistus comes from the extremely critical writings of St. Hippolytus, a leading and highly learned Roman theologian and presbyter (priest), who was severely disapproving of the Roman pontificate around this time.

✝ ✝ ✝

Aside from probably not being a martyr, Callistus was also a criminal.

Although not born a Christian, in his youth Callistus had been a slave to a Roman Christian who agreed to set him up in

banking if the boy accepted the faith. Callistus readily did so and was soon running a substantial banking business that dealt only with Christian customers. However, it turns out that Callistus was fleecing them all. When he was found out, his banking operation was shut down, and Callistus fled.

One year later, Callistus returned to Rome and became embroiled in a fight in a synagogue during the Jewish Sabbath that allegedly left a man injured. He was arrested and brought to trial, where his previous sharp dealings in banking may have counted against him. Convicted and sentenced to hard labor in the Sardinian salt mines, Callistus, although still nominally a Christian, was widely regarded as a violent and bullying inmate. However, this did not stop him from using his faith to join a group of Christian prisoners petitioning the emperor's Christian mistress, Maria, for release. The petition was successful and Callistus was released. He later found out that the current pope, Victor I, had objected to his release because of his criminal activities and violent conduct and deliberately excluded him from the list submitted to the Emperor. Callistus only succeeded because he'd had the foresight to also petition the prison governor—the only prisoner to do so at the time—and he was released under the governor's dispensation.

Upon his second return to Rome, Callistus loudly professed

his Christianity and, unaware of the papal enmity toward him, asked Pope Victor to appoint him as an officer of the Roman Church. Victor refused and instead sent him to Anzio to live on a yearly pension. ✦ Anzio: a city in the Lazio region of Italy. ✦ Victor's successor, the weak and vacillating Zephrynus, recalled Callistus to Rome and installed him as his own deacon with special responsibility for the churches within the Roman diocese. This gave Callistus immense power, as well as the pope's ear. Callistus was able to easily manipulate Zephrynus, even getting the ailing pontiff to name him as his successor. Upon the death of the pope, Callistus was elected—to the fury of many Roman theologians, including St. Hippolytus.

✂ ST. HIPPOLYTUS AS THE ANTIPOPE? ✂

The prominent writer and priest St. Hippolytus, aware that the new pope had used his position in the Church to enhance his personal wealth, refused to accept the election of Callistus, going so far as to name him the first antipope. ✦ Antipope: one who sits in opposition to the pope but who claims full papal authority. ✦ Because he temporarily broke off from the church and led his own assemblage, Hippolytus himself is sometimes considered the first antipope. He reconciled with the church before dying a martyr, however, and later became the patron saint of horses.

Most of his five-year pontificate was spent fighting with Hippolytus as well as other Roman theologians and their followers. Callistus managed to survive their attempts to dethrone him by claiming their accusations were merely hearsay, and perhaps he bribed some factions of the Roman citizenry to earn their support.

A tomb was designated to Callistus on the Appian Way, but for a long time after his death, his burial place was kept hidden. ✦ Appian Way: the Via Appia, one of the most important roads in the ancient Roman Republic, connecting Rome with Brindisi and Apulia in southeast Italy. ✦ The reason for such secrecy, it is assumed, was to prevent the tomb from being desecrated by the followers of Hippolytus. In 1960, his grave was discovered in a concealed but ornate tomb in the cemetery of Calepodius on the Via Aurelia, hidden under an oratory erected by Pope Julius I in the fourth century. The tomb itself was elaborately decorated, depicting Callistus as a martyr—although it is doubtful that he was. The tomb may have even been paid for with the monies Callistus had stolen from his Christian clients in his early days as a banker.

BOGUS POPES

Even though there is a proper election system in place, sometimes, somehow, someone else ends up in Peter's chair. Marcellus I and Boniface II are two such cases. While Marecellus I's rise to pope is shrouded in mystery, it is clear that Boniface II took the chair through an illegitimate election.

Marcellus I (November/December 306–January 308)
Who was he and why was he so vicious?

The legitimacy of several popes is open to question, but the pontificate of Marcellus I must rank among the most dubious. Who was he? When did he reign? Was he actually a churchman? For instance, Marcellus is not mentioned in Eusebius of Caesarea's famous history of the church and its popes, the *Annuario Pontificio*. ✦ *Annuario Pontificio*: the Vatican's official directory of popes. ✦ The *Annuario Pontificio* gives his dates as May/June 308–January 309, but some sources say he might have governed the Church as early as 304. To further complicate the picture, he's often confused with his predecessor, Marcellinus. What is *not* open to question, however, is that few popes were as openly vicious and vindictive as Marcellus. Indeed, he was so vicious that the Roman Emperor Maxentius was forced to banish him from the city as a disturber of the peace.

In 303, during the reign of Marcellinus, Roman Emperor Diocletian launched a persecution against all Christians. A weak and impotent pope, Marcellinus complied with the Emperor's demands to hand over all copies of sacred scripture to the Roman authorities and to publicly burn incense as an offering to the Roman gods.

✝✝✝

During the slaughter that marked Diocletian's reign as emperor, many Christians lapsed in their faith and worshipped Roman gods.

✝✝✝

This has led some Church historians to believe that he had abdicated the papacy before his death and that Marcellus may have taken the helm around 304.

But who was Marcellus exactly? He is described in the *Annuario Pontificio* as "a leading presbyter (priest) in the pontificate of Marcellinus," but it is unclear as to where he might have preached. Indeed, it has been suggested that he was Marcellinus's son and that he may not even have been a churchman—some believe he was a nominally Christian soldier who assumed power because of his bloodline to Marcellinus.

The Diocletian persecutions together with divisions in the Church may have delayed the election of Marcellinus's succes-

sor for up to three years, giving Marcellus time to consolidate his position and force the clergy to accept him as their leader. He was determined to repair the fractured Church—which had been almost decimated by the Christian persecutions and internal feuding—and to punish its detractors. Those who had compromised their beliefs, he ruled, were to be hunted down and put to death as heretics and backsliders. Those who unreservedly repented and submitted themselves to the papal rule might be spared, but they were to receive the severest penance for the good of their immortal souls.

Marcellus's own persecution was so vicious that it provoked a backlash against Christianity in Rome, resulting in riots and bloodshed on the streets. The new Emperor Maxentius was forced to intervene in order to avoid full-scale public disorder. He banished Marcellus from the city. At first, the pope refused to go and seemed willing to stand up to the Emperor. He did eventually leave, and may have later abdicated. In any case, he is thought to have died shortly after his expulsion. His body was later brought back to Rome and, despite his vicious behavior, he was canonized. Even today, much about his identity remains a mystery, and nobody really knows if his claim to the pontificate was genuine.

Boniface II (September 22, 530–October 17, 532)
Legitimate election not necessary?

In order for a pope to hold a legitimate claim on the papacy, he must be elected by a majority of cardinals. In early Rome, this election also usually needed the support of the Roman people, but it was the cardinals and churchmen who had the final say. In the case of Boniface II, it was a little different.

Although born in Rome, Boniface was of German stock. He had served as archdeacon under one of his predecessors, John I, and continued in that capacity during the pontificate of his immediate predecessor, Felix IV (III), but with greatly increased powers. When Boniface was summoned to the dying pontiff's sickbed, along with a number of Roman senators and several members of the army, Felix offered up his pallium and allegedly named Boniface as his successor. ✦ Pallium: a woolen garment worn around the neck as a symbol of pastoral authority. ✦ This gesture broke with both political and spiritual law—God alone knew who the papal successor would be, and all discussion of it was forbidden during the lifetime of a sitting pope. There is no doubt, however, that Boniface was incredibly ambitious and saw himself as the next pope. The Roman Senate, unwilling to see a German take the papal throne instead of a Roman, moved to stop him.

When Felix finally died, the cardinals met in the Lateran Basilica and, under direction from the Senate, elected the deacon Dioscorus of Alexandria—a Roman churchman—as their next pope. ✦ Lateran: the Lateran Palace, residence of the popes incorporating St. John Lateran, the Cathedral of Rome. ✦ Dioscorus had been a confidant of two previous popes— Symmachus (498–514) and Hormisdas (514–523)—and was regarded as a competent administrator. However, in an adjacent hall, another faction elected Boniface. Although this group included some churchmen, it was largely a lay and military faction that had no real authority to elect a pope. Both popes were consecrated on the same day, September 22, by rival bishops, and each denounced the other as a heretic.

According to Cannon Law, it was Dioscorus who had been properly elected and it was he who had the legitimate authority. However, his reign lasted only twenty-two days—he died under mysterious circumstances. As the cardinals assembled in the Lateran to elect his successor, Boniface suddenly showed up, backed by a military faction of his followers, and demanded that they now fully proclaim him pope. When the cardinals protested, Boniface threatened to turn his military loose, vowing that none of them would leave the Lateran alive. In a sudden flash of divine inspiration, the cardinals realized he'd been right

all along and unanimously proclaimed him pope. Boniface's first act was to declare the unfortunate Dioscorus an antipope and a heretic and order his name stricken from all Vatican documents.

✝✝✝

Even today, Dioscorus remains absent from all official records.

✝✝✝

History would remember *him*, not his rival. All those who spoke out against him were threatened with military action or death. And, as the Roman Senate had feared, Boniface set about establishing a Germanic line in the papacy, to the exclusion of any Roman influence. He tried to ensure that his successor would find favor with the East German Goths, and especially with the Ostrogothic King Athalaric. To this end, he nominated the pro-German deacon Vigilus for the papacy. The Roman Senate moved quickly, demanding that he change his nomination, and once again Boniface threatened them with the army. However, this time the fear of the Germans proved too much and he had little support from military quarters; he was forced to renounce the nomination and to publicly burn the document naming Vigilus as his successor—a truly humiliating experience for such an egotistical pope. Boniface died, largely unmourned, in October 532, leaving behind a Church in turbulence and confusion.

MARRIED POPES

Hormisdas (July 20, 514–August 6, 523) and many more

Popes are celibate, right? Well, this hasn't always been the case. In the early days of the church, the clergy were not required to be unmarried and, although it was a mark of hermits, monks, and aesthetics, it has been suggested that in the first 1,200 years of the papacy, there were at least thirty-nine popes who were married or had been married at one time. Although it was the custom for unmarried popes to remain that way upon election, celibacy was considered an alternative lifestyle and individual choice. In fact, some popes were the undisputed fathers of subsequent pontiffs. Pope Hormisdas, for example, was the father of one of his successors, Pope Silverius (536–537), who may have been married himself; Gregory I (590–604), or Gregory the Great, is thought to have been the great-grandson of Felix III (II) (483–492). Some popes, such as Hormisdas, were already widowers before they ascended to the papal throne. Others, however, had partners and refused calls to "put away their wives," citing the example of the first pope, St. Simon Peter, who kept his wife and family with him.

Perhaps one of the more famous of the married popes was Hadrian (Adrian) II (867–872). A respected churchman, Adrian had been offered the papacy twice and had refused it both times—on the third time he accepted, although the exact date of his election is unknown. Adrian had a wife and a daughter, whom he brought to live with him in the Lateran Palace where special apartments were created for them. The criticism of the married pope was fierce among his political enemies, including the Duke of Spoleto—and there was danger awaiting Adrian and his family in the Vatican.

Upon the death of Leo IV in 855, a faction within the church elected the Vatican librarian Anastasius as his successor. As most of the church considered this election invalid, Anastasius was quickly deposed and Benedict III was installed. The former antipope continued on as librarian through the reign of Nicholas I (858–867). However, he still harbored ambitions to be pope, and when Adrian became pontiff, he made his move. Perhaps

at the urging of the Duke of Spoleto, Anastasius began to stir up some resentment around the new pope and his marriage. The Spoletan army attacked Rome and, in the confusion, Anastasius's brother Eleutherius entered the Lateran and took Adrian's wife and daughter prisoner. While in captivity, the pope's daughter was raped and murdered; and when her mother tried to intervene, she suffered the same fate. Distraught, Adrian appealed to the French King Louis II for help in tracking down the kidnappers and murderers. The brutal incident was also too much for the Roman people, who backed Adrian and helped him overthrow the rebels. Anastasius, who was believed to be behind the whole incident, was stripped of his office, excommunicated, and banished from the city. However, a year later Adrian brought him back and reinstated him in another position in the chancery. The whole tragic episode served as a warning to the papacy that marriage was not acceptable in the Roman Church, or else they risk putting their families in danger.

Silverius (536–537), was another pope who may have been married. He is known to have lived in the Lateran Palace with a woman named Antonia, but whether or not she was actually his wife is open to debate. It did not, however, stop him from being canonized as a saint.

During the medieval period, the idea of mandatory celibacy for all clergy—including popes—came to the fore. The monastic ideal of abstaining from the worldly pleasures of the flesh took a hold on the religious mind, and clerics were expected to comply and remain chaste. Of course, this did not stop some pontiffs from taking wives and keeping them secret. Only one pope is thought to have married while in office, Boniface IX (1389–1404).

✝ ✝ ✝

Boniface IX, a pope of the Great Western Schism, (see page 151) is reputed to have annulled any doctrine relating to the pontiff's celibacy so he could marry his mistress. Boniface behaved like an autocrat and dictator throughout his reign, and no one dared question him on the matter.

✝ ✝ ✝

The French pontiff Clement IV (1265–1268) was also certainly married, although it's unclear whether his wife was alive when he was elected. The antipope Felix V (1439–1449), who served as pope before being deposed by Nicholas V (1447–1455), had formerly been Amadeus, Duke of Savoy and already had a wife before he was elected. He was the last of the antipopes and, to the best of current knowledge, the last of the popes to be officially married.

Many single popes were not above keeping mistresses or consorting with married women. John XII, for instance, is believed to have had a severe and ultimately fatal stroke while in the bed of a married woman (see page 77). The full extent of papal philandering will likely remain a mystery, as the Vatican keeps these secrets closely guarded in the archives.

RACKETEER POPE
Sabinian (September 13, 604–February 22, 606)

Arguably the most hated pope in history, Sabinian reversed much of the legislation passed by his powerful predecessor, the reformer Gregory I, and promoted several rather dubious characters to the clergy. At the time of his elevation, Rome was besieged by the Lombards and also suffering from one in a series of periodic famines. ✦ Lombards: a Germanic people from northeast Europe. ✦ With food in short supply, Sabinian used some of the Church funds to procure grain for the city. The population hailed him as a savior, but the pope had another agenda. He immediately set up a racketeering network involving some of the city's criminals, and they distributed the grain at black-market prices. He pocketed the proceeds himself; those who spoke out against him were promptly excommunicated or beaten up by his criminal confederates.

Sabinian ignored the public's hostility and even the riots that broke out against him. When he died in February 606, his funeral procession had to make a detour outside the city walls in order to avoid mobs who were *still* rioting against the unpopular pope. He was accused of black-market trading, racketeering, and profiting from the misfortunes of Rome. Had the mob laid

their hands on his body, they would have torn it to pieces. For the same reason, the location of his grave—somewhere in the Lateran—remains a secret to this day.

MENTALLY FRAIL POPE
Conon (October 21, 686–September 22, 687)

In the history of the papacy, there have been several "compromise" or "stop-gap" figures—in other words, popes who took office until a more suitable candidate emerged or to hold together radically opposed factions within the Church. The ancient Conon, elected in 686, was such a figure.

At the time of his election, the Roman Church was badly divided. Certain political and military factions had realized that gaining control of religious institutions would allow them greater power; so they set out to wrest it from the priests. In 686, two distinct factions emerged: one, headed by the archpriest Peter, supported a more spiritual role and favored control of the Church by the ordained clergy; the other, headed by the priest Theodore, was backed by several local militias eager to seize power. Moreover, the papacy itself was in decline. A series of short-term pontiffs left the Church without a sense of continuity or purpose. The last, John V (July 685–August 686), had ruled for just over a year and was ill most of that time. His predecessor Benedict II (June 684–May 685) had been only slightly more effective but failed to do much during his eleven-month pontificate. Consequently, the split between the clergy and the military factions had grown.

The Church's two factions met immediately following the death of John V on August 2, 686, but no successor was named. Talks continued on and off for two months, until one day, as Peter's faction left the Lateran, Theodore's military group suddenly moved in, sealing off the chapel and allowing none of the clergy back in. They planned to elect a pope of their own.

In desperation, the clergy put forward an old and ailing cleric named Conon. His father had been a general in the Roman army, and the churchmen hoped that this would make him appealing to the military faction. The idea worked, and Conon was elected as a compromise candidate.

There is no doubt that Conon was extremely old and in poor health.

✝ ✝ ✝

According to some accounts, Conon may have been in the initial stages of what is now known as Alzheimer's disease.

✝ ✝ ✝

Although he had moments of great clarity, there were reportedly times when he didn't even know he was pope. He is described in some accounts as "simple-minded;" however, various historians have taken this to mean that he was a man of simple tastes and a saintly demeanor. Nevertheless, he seems to have been kept away

from the public gaze, and only one or two things are known about his actual pontificate. Any decisions that he appears to have made were disastrous, leading to the assumption that he might have been mentally incompetent.

Conon's most glaring error was the nomination of the deacon of the Church in Syracuse, an incredibly lucrative post that was normally reserved for a senior member of the Roman clergy. Instead, Conon handed it to a Sicilian who was known to be of somewhat dubious character. He also allowed him exclusive use of the ceremonial saddlecloths normally reserved for the Romans, as well as several other "perks." It was very clear that the pope did not know with whom he was dealing—the appointee used his position to extort money out of local businesses and lands owned by the Church in Syracuse. When the papal tenants complained directly to the pope, he sent them back a stinging letter telling them to behave themselves and respect the Church. The deacon was, after all, his appointee. Thus, the tenants rioted and the deacon was arrested and deported by the governor of Sicily. Conon, however, continued to write to him as if he were still in office.

In the final months of his life, Conon was "continuously ill" and no one was allowed to see him, save for a few Cardinals. He

died late in September 686 and was buried in St. Peter's, but the method of his election and the general perception of his reign had left the Church bitterly divided. This would all be left for his successor, the much stronger-willed and authoritarian Sergius I, to sort out.

GETTING ELECTED

In order to understand how some of these individuals actually managed to become pope, it is first necessary to know how the Church identifies its apostolic succession.

✝ ✝ ✝

Even though the pope claims to be a direct successor of the Apostle Peter, he is not chosen in any mystical way, as is, say, the Dalai Lama. Rather, he is chosen by political means, which, like many other such processes, might be open to manipulation and even corruption.

✝ ✝ ✝

The pope is elected by a conclave of cardinals who are said to vote under the direct inspiration of God, the implication being that the individual elected is, in fact, God's choice. ✦ Conclave: from the Latin "cum clave," or with key. For the past five centuries, it has been the tradition of the cardinals to lock themselves in the Sistine Chapel until they come to an agreement about who will be the next pope. ✦ This may not always be the case. The problem is that, historically, the Church is roughly composed of two elements—the spiritual (priests, bishops) and the secular or "Princes of the Church" (cardinals, monsignors), with the secular arm electing the head of the spiritual

arm. In past centuries, this has tainted the proceedings with "worldliness," or unholiness, making them susceptible to allegations of impropriety.

In the early Christian world, *congregations* were responsible for the election of their own clergy. Therefore, for the first thousand or so years of the Church's history, popes were elected solely by the bishops and citizenry of Rome. In the sixth and seventh centuries, however, the clergies of neighboring diocese began to take an increasing interest in the election of the Bishop of Rome. Politically, Rome was slowly starting to reemerge as a local power, and churchmen realized that part of that power and influence might lie within the bishopric. Additionally, influential laypersons, such as civil and military officials and wealthy families, also noted the rebirth of Rome and began to plan accordingly. Influence over the bishop of a politically developing diocese would advance their plans considerably. Even so, the approval of the Roman populace was always deemed necessary.

Theoretically, the Church and State still remained totally separate, but in practice they were fast becoming intertwined. From the time of the Byzantine conquest of Northern Italy and Sicily around AD 535–53, Eastern emperors had tried to

force the outcome of papal elections with military threats and bribery. Things were no better at the end of the eighth century, when both political power and approval for the papacy shifted from the Byzantines to the Lombards and then to the Franks. By the time Leo III was elected in 795, the Frankish Emperor Charlemagne demanded not only notification of the election of the pope but also the keys to St. Peter's tomb and the papal banner of Rome as recognition of the Emperor's sovereignty over the Holy See. In an attempt to cut out imperial interference in elections, a Roman synod convened under Pope Stephen III (IV) determined that only clergy were entitled to vote in papal elections and that the office of pope could only be ratified by the Church itself. ✦ Synod: a council of the Church determining doctrine. ✦

The policy changes were only partly successful and they did not keep wealthy families from interfering in the elections. The pope's position was rapidly becoming more temporal in nature, with the Holy See acquiring lands in its own right. Although originally a spiritual office, many pontiffs were starting to behave like worldly rulers themselves, dispensing lands and favors in the manner of an earthly monarch. Many important Roman families could afford bribes and gifts in order to secure

the papacy for their candidates. In some cases, both political and financial ambitions intertwined, and families and factions competed for the papal position in a most unedifying manner, such as the events that surrounded the astonishing Cadaver Synod in 897 (see page 55).

✂ MULTIPLE POPES ✂

Failure to win an election did not always stop candidates from becoming pope. If, for example, someone had sufficient local, financial, or—more important—military and political backing, he could simply declare himself pope and excommunicate the incumbent. This led to a phenomenon known as the *antipope* (of which there were several) and to the rather astonishing spectacle of two—and in one case, *three*—pontiffs, each with his own set of followers and declaring the other a heretic. Fortunately for the organization of the Church, these circumstances were infrequent, although antipopes did present a major ongoing problem during what became known as "The Western Schism" (see page 151).

During the fifteenth and sixteenth centuries, the papacy was mired in controversy, corruption, and outright sleaze. Backed by both wealthy families and political might, the popes were

acting more or less as worldly rulers with scant regard for the sacredness of their calling. The system of bribes and favors by which many of them were elected was seeping down into the Church as a whole—scoundrels, madmen, and hedonists often rose to power, and some popes were hastily elected just to avoid potential riots by Roman citizens. Eventually, the corruption encouraged a revolt against the Catholic hierarchy and ultimately led to the formation of Protestantism.

Today, elections to the pontificate are more regulated, circumspect affairs. And yet, some will say that such corruption is still present in the process, as evidenced by "events" that sometimes occur after an unpopular election—for instance, the alleged 1978 murder of John Paul I. While we may think the more turbulent papal times have passed, who knows what may happen in the future?

DEAD POPE
Stephen II (March 22–March 24, 752)

Given that Stephen II may not have actually been alive during his reign, it's no wonder that even the *Annuario Pontificio* lists conflicting dates for it. In some extracts, Stephen is given three days in March 752, while others say he lasted from March 22, 752 to April 26, 757. Nor can the records agree on Stephen's exact numbering—some call him Stephen II, others Stephen III. The official Vatican records call him Stephen II (III) and display all subsequent popes named Stephen with dual numbering. Might this mean that *another* pope named Stephen took over when the first one died? What *is* clear is that there was great debate throughout the Church over whether or not Stephen II was ever consecrated as pope. Nor is there any agreement about his death or about what happened during his reign. Some accounts say that at the end of three days, the Holy Father died from a "fatal seizure" (possibly a heart attack), while others say he simply suffered an attack that left him incapacitated. The former accounts state that he issued no papal decrees during a brief pontificate; the latter accounts claim that he issued letters to Pepin and even met with the Frankish king. Whatever the truth of it, Stephen II does not appear to have been very active, and this has led to

suggestions that Roman authorities might have staged a "cover up" for political purposes—maybe one so extreme as creating a substitute pope.

If the fatal seizure story is true, it's possible that Stephen died during his coronation. At the time, Rome was under threat from the Lombard king Aistulf, who was intent on conquering most of Italy. Aistulf had just declared the city part of his territories and issued a demand for a tax on all its citizens. When a number of Roman subjects refused to pay, many began to fear that the Lombard king would attack. In order to defend itself, Rome needed an alliance with another monarch, and the only person who could command any sort of authority with other rulers was the pope, Zachary (741–752). However, just as attack seemed imminent, Pope Zachary died. A replacement pope had to be found, and quickly.

The cardinals made their choice in haste—an elderly priest who was rushed to the Lateran and declared Stephen II. The celebrations of the day and the impending strain of office may have proved too much for the old man, leading to that fatal attack. With the Lombards at the gate and a reply expected from Emperor Constantine in the east (with whom Stephen's predecessors had tried to form an alliance), it would have

been disastrous to announce that the pontiff had died. And so Stephen was allowed to reign for three days, even though he was dead. Because the old priest was not widely known, the cardinals could substitute someone else for him. According to one story, this new pope was unanimously but secretly elected in St. Mary Major Basilica, and he took over for the dead pope immediately, also taking the name Stephen.

When the letter to the Emperor in Constantinople went unanswered (perhaps he'd taken umbrage at the developing split between the Eastern and Western Churches), Pope Stephen appealed directly to Pepin, the King of the Franks. Pepin said he would consider aiding Rome if the pope appeared before him in person at his court in Ponthion. Of course, he had never seen the new pope and didn't know what he looked like. In the height of winter, *someone* traveled with a retinue across the Alps to Pepin's court—the first pope to allegedly make that journey. When the travelers arrived, they appeared before the Frankish king in penitential rags, threw themselves at his feet, and begged him in the name of St. Peter to help them against the Lombards. Slightly taken aback by the unusually humble behavior, Pepin not only promised to help, but gave this agreement in writing; he placed this document into the hands of the man he thought was the pope.

There was, however, one more wrinkle to the story. According to the Abbot of Saint-Denis, who tended to the sick pontiff, at that moment Stephen II was lying gravely ill in the monastery of Saint-Denis outside Paris. He had contracted a fever while crossing the Alps and now lay on his deathbed. Could the Church have elected *two* backup Stephen IIs to ensure that the mission to Pepin was successful? Whatever the truth, the pope returned to full health by July 754, when he formally anointed Pepin and his wife, thus establishing the Carolingian dynasty. Clearly, this had to be the same man Pepin met in Ponthion.

✝ ✝ ✝

The pope bestowed on Pepin the title "Patrician of the Romans," implying that he was a holy defender of the city.

✝ ✝ ✝

The Franks crossed the Alps and attacked the Lombard forces, decisively crushing Aistulf, who then sued for peace. A broken agreement and second crushing defeat later, Aistulf died without a legitimate heir. The Lombard threat now gone, Pepin handed over to the pope lands he had captured in battle, which until then had been under the control of the Byzantine Emperor Constantine. When Constantine protested, Pepin replied that he was answerable to nobody but St. Peter and the pope, whoever

that might be. With this acquisition of land, the pope became a temporal ruler as well as a spiritual one—a mixed blessing.

Although it had played only a small part in the whole affair, the papacy fared very well out of it, considering the pope was probably dead and had been so for a number of years. According to some sources, Stephen officially "died" in 757 and was buried in St. Peters. For centuries, the Vatican maintained that the man who died was the same man who had been elected on March 22, 752, but twelve centuries later offered a grudging admission of uncertainty by renumbering the papal title Stephen II (III) and giving all subsequent popes of the same name a dual numbering. Even today, the matter remains ambiguous. However, as some might point out, why be so coy about an affair that gives added status to the papacy? Not only can popes achieve a great deal in life—they can sometimes achieve even more when dead!

"FALSE POPE"
Stephen III (IV) (August 7, 768–January 24, 772)

Few popes have come to the papacy in such trying, violent circumstances and have had as unhappy a reign as Stephen III (IV).

Before Stephen, the severe and rigidly administrative Paul I had dreadfully alienated the Roman lay nobility from the Church. They considered murdering Paul but their plot was uncovered and the pope died shortly afterward. Hoping to find a pontiff who would be more sympathetic to their needs and interests, they formed a pact with the electing cardinals to choose someone who would work closely with both the Roman aristocracy and business. However, one of the cardinals violated the agreement and had his own brother, Constantine, (who was not even a churchman) proclaimed as pope by a mob of soldiers. He was installed in the Lateran, ordained as a deacon, and consecrated as pontiff in St. Peter's Basilica by three bishops held at the point of a sword wielded by a drunken soldier. Constantine immediately wrote to Pepin III, King of the Franks, informing him of his "election," but the Frankish king made no reply.

As alliances shifted, Lombard troops, opposed to the election, entered Rome and incited fighting in the streets. Constantine's brother and chief supporter was killed during

hand-to-hand fighting, and Constantine himself fled the papal throne and hid in the Lateran oratory where he was soon found and arrested. The Lombards swiftly elected their own pope—a chaplain at a local monastery named Philip. As the Lombard troops started to withdraw, the Roman mob turned on the new pope; the cardinals refused to recognize his election, and the unfortunate Philip was booted out of the Lateran to be torn apart by the mob. The powerful chief notary of the Holy See, Christopher, anxious for power himself, saw to it that Stephen was elected by a majority of cardinals, and he took the throne on August 1, 768. The agreement between the two men stipulated that, in return for a guaranteed election, Stephen would name Christopher as his successor.

However, the former "Pope" Constantine was still at large and able to make mischief. In an attempt to raise the Romans against Stephen, Constantine denounced him as a "false pope" and drew attention to the rumored pact with his notary. Some of the army supported him, but not enough. After several days of bloody fighting, Constantine was dragged from his hiding place and paraded through the city, then imprisoned in a local monastery. When a mob attacked the monastery, Constantine was beaten and his eyes were gouged out.

Hearing of his rival's misfortune, Stephen gave a public prayer of thanks and ordered that all records of Constantine's election and his edicts be burned—acts that Stephen, as a member of Constantine's College of Cardinals, had personally signed. He declared Constantine an antipope and himself the Vicar of Christ, even though Constantine's consecration, while illicit, had been totally valid. In fact, Stephen himself was a usurper. Nevertheless, a synod convened by the notary Christopher confirmed him as pope and further decreed that the laity should no longer have any say in papal elections.

†††

His rise to power complete, Stephen sent an envoy to Pepin III to inform him that he was now pope. He also invited Frankish bishops to attend a synod that would depose the edicts of the "false Pope" Constantine; thirteen bishops traveled to Rome for the occasion. However, the synod descended into a morass of political intrigue, back-biting, maneuvering, and horse-trading, with scant regard for any sort of religious conformity.

†††

Although he had given Christopher his word that he would name him the next pope, Stephen had no intention of doing so. In fact, now that he was elected, he intended to get rid of the notary alto-

gether. He conspired with Desiderius, King of the Lombards, to have Christopher and his son Sergius murdered. Then he wrote to the new Frankish king Charlemagne, creating an elaborate lie about the circumstances of their deaths: he said Christopher and his son had been planning to murder *him*, and that Desiderius had saved him. Desiderius knew what he was up to and saw an opportunity for blackmail—soon Stephen was little more than a tool of the Lombard monarch. In 771, disagreements broke out between Charlemagne and Desiderius; when the former refused to acknowledge the marriage of his daughter to the Lombard ruler (a marriage that Stephen had backed), relations with the papacy deteriorated even further. Stephen had blundered his way to a papal court now riddled with indecision, double-dealing, and intrigue. With his reign in tatters, Stephen III (IV) died on January 24, 772, and was buried in St. Peter's. The reign of this "false pope" had been both a shambles and a failure.

ROBBER POPE
Sergius II (January 844–January 847)

Few pontificates have been as openly corrupt as that of Sergius II. Irascible and gouty, he assumed the papal throne sometime in late January 844. Prior to taking office, he had been almost universally disliked as the cardinal-priest at the church of Santi Martino e Silvestro ai Monti and was obviously not a popular choice for pope. Plus, the Roman people had already enthroned a likeable deacon named John as the next pontiff. Sergius, however, had other ideas, and with the backing and military force of the Roman aristocracy he quickly expelled John from the Lateran, installing himself as pope.

✝ ✝ ✝

John, the people's choice, did try to rally his supporters until Sergius threatened him with excommunication and death unless he went quietly—which, in the end, is what he did.

✝ ✝ ✝

Faced with the threat of rebellion, Sergius was hastily elected without the formal acknowledgment of the Frankish court, which was required by the Roman Constitution of 824. In retaliation to this public snub, Frankish emperor Lothair sent his son Louis to Italy with an army that plundered papal lands and threatened the

city of Rome. On the outskirts of the city, Louis halted and ordered a papal council to investigate the pope's election. Already one step ahead, Sergius managed to rig the council with placed men whom he had bribed, threatened, or blackmailed to find in his favor.

Now that he was safely installed in office, the pope and his brother Benedict began a career of extortion and robbery. Although he was certainly not the first pope to be in cahoots with Roman criminals, Sergius's involvement ran very deep. It is believed that at one point the pope controlled most of the gambling and prostitution in the city and that he was personally connected to a number of murders within the precincts of Rome. Supposedly, he took out "contracts," or paid assassinations, on many of his opponents.

✂ FOR THE GLORY OF GOD ✂

So corrupt and weak had the Roman papacy become that its enemies took full advantage of the situation. In 846, a large eet of Saracen pirates successfully attacked and thoroughly plundered St. Peter's and St. Paul's, carrying off treasures and relics. Sergius had been repeatedly warned about such an event but had done nothing to prevent it. The attack was therefore seen by many as God's judgment upon Rome in response to papal corruption, and public anger finally turned on Sergius. However, he died six months later and was buried in St. Peter's; few mourned his passing.

FEMALE POPE

John VIII? (855–858? or December 14, 872–December 16, 882?)

Throughout medieval history and beyond, the legend of "Pope Joan" was handed down from one generation to the next. In many versions, the figure of the female pontiff is associated with the reign of John VIII, even though her dates (roughly 855–58) were before his ten-year reign, which began in 872.

These dates *do* coincide with the reign of another pope, Benedict III (September 29, 855–April 17, 858), about whom very little is known. It seems unlikely that a female could have kept her gender secret during an ongoing power struggle with an antipope, Anastasius, and while imprisoned in the Lateran Palace, which we know occurred during Benedict III's reign. There were stories saying Benedict did not reign at all, but that on the death of Leo IV, a cardinal named John Angelicus (John the Angel) was elevated to the papacy—and "*he*" was a woman! When this was discovered, the pope was immediately removed from office and executed. "His" name was struck from the Vatican records and Benedict III stepped in as the replacement pope. The whole thing, according to some historians, was nothing more than a Vatican cover-up.

✝✝✝

Could a woman have ascended to St. Peter's chair without anyone noticing? In an age when few people washed or even changed their clothes, it might not have been as unlikely as it sounds. Furthermore, an austere and withdrawn pope might have discouraged those nearby from examining him too closely.

✝✝✝

The most popular legend of Pope Joan goes like this: An English or German woman made her way to Rome via Athens disguised as a monk, calling herself John Angelicus. After a brilliant career in Vatican circles, she was unanimously elevated to the papacy, allegedly taking the name John VIII. According to many traditions, she was quite sexually promiscuous during her two-and-a-half-year reign. During an Easter procession near the Basilica of San Clemente, she was suddenly taken ill and fell to the pavement. The reason for her discomfort soon became clear, as she gave birth in front of the astonished cardinals, thus revealing her true gender. Immediately following the birth, she was torn limb from limb by an outraged Roman mob. Other versions say she was imprisoned and later stoned to death. All references to her reign were expunged by her successor in an act of *damnatio memoriae*. ✦ Damnatio memoriae: literally, "damnation of memory;" removal from remembrance. ✦

Another source of the legend may lie in the debauched reign of John XII (see "The Promiscuous Pope," page 77), who allegedly enjoyed dressing as a woman from time to time. And he does not seem to have been the only pope to do so. Julius III (see "The Gay Pope," page 172) and Paul II may also have been cross-dressers. Perhaps these personalities gave rise to the idea of a female pontiff.

There are, however, historians who claim that the Catholic Church accepted this female pope long after her death. According to their accounts, her child (a boy) was raised by the priesthood and later became bishop of Ostia. A statue, they say, was erected in her memory and called "The Woman Pope and her Child;" it depicted a pontiff in full robes, bestowing a blessing but with a child in her

arms. There are disputes as to its location, but some say it stood on the Vicus Papissa ("the street of the woman Pope"), which still exists today. In 1601, however, Pope Clement XIII is said to have demanded that the statue be pulled down and replaced with one of Pope Zacharias, thus eliminating all imagery of the female pontiff.

Other writers, such as the fourteenth century poet Giovanni Boccaccio and the fifteenth century writer Adam of Usk also mention the female pontiff.

The lack of a real, authoritative account of a female pope might suggest that the Vatican destroyed all records. Thus, her story remains a mystery.

However, her alleged reign *has* led to another intriguing piece of papal folklore—the *sedes stircoria,* a throne on which newly elected popes were required to sit in order to confirm their masculinity. According to legend, before consecration was complete, an elected pope sat on the throne—which had a large hole in its center—without any undergarments. A cardinal, specially appointed for the occasion and in full view of the electing cardinals, would feel underneath to be sure that the pontiff was masculine. When the cry *"Testicules habit"* ("he has testicles") was heard, everybody joyfully proceeded to the consecration. It is said that Pius XII was the last pope to submit himself to such an indignity.

✂ WRITINGS ON THE FEMALE POPE ✂

Altogether, a female pope is mentioned in five hundred accounts.
Here are a few of the most notable:

NAME	PROFESSION, CENTURY	WORK	TYPE OF REFERENCE
Anastasius Bibliothecius	Writer, ninth century	*Liber Pontificalis (Book of Popes)*	Margin note (may have been added later)
Marianus Scotus	Chronicler, eleventh century	*Chronicle of the Popes*	Reference to a female pontiff
Stephen of Bourbon	Writer and historian, thirteenth century	*De Septum Domis Spiritus Sancti (The Seven Gifts of the Holy Spirit)*	Tells the story of a female who, under the devil's in uence, became pope, gave birth, and was stoned to death
Martin Polonus (von Troppau)	Polish chronicler and archbishop of Gnesen, thirteenth century	*Chronicon Pontificum et Imperatum (The Chronicle of the Popes and Emperors)*	Details the Pope's name as "Johanna" (Joanna) or "Joan" (the name seems to change to "John" in *Chronicon Pontificum et Imperatum*)
Jean de Mailley	French Dominican chronicler, thirteenth century	*Chronica Universalis Mettenis (A Universal History of Metz)*	Records the story as fact but dates it around 1099

†††

Photographs of a gender-verification throne are dismissed by the Vatican as showing not a *sedes stircoria*, but a bidet or birthing chair used by women.

†††

Today, the Church maintains that the story of a female pontiff was no more than Protestant propaganda, circulated in the sixteenth century to discredit the Catholic Church as corrupt and gullible. (Nevermind that the tales of Pope Joan stretch much farther back than the Protestant Reformation.) Regardless, she remains an intriguing figure both within and beyond the Church.

EXHUMED POPE
Formosus (October 6, 891–April 4, 896)

As colorful, intelligent, and troubled as Pope Formosus was in life, he is more memorable for what happened after his death. The ghoulish Cadavar Synod—which involved dressing up Formosus's exhumed rotting cadaver and conducting a post-mortem trial—clearly says more about the pope who orchestrated this horror-fiction-sounding scene, Stephen VI (VII), than it does about the dead pope himself.

In 896, at the age of eighty, Formosus died and was interred with due ceremony in St. Peter's. His successor was Boniface VI, who only reigned for a matter of weeks. Boniface's successor, Stephen VI (VII), was not only mentally unstable but also extremely close to Lambert, Duke of Spoleto—Formosus's old adversary. Perhaps at the promptings of Lambert and his family, Stephen convened the astonishing and gruesome Cadaver Synod (the *Synod Horrenda*) in January 897, nine months after Formosus's death. Summoning a conclave of cardinals, who were forced to attend under pain of death, Stephen exhumed the body of the dead pope, dressed it in full pontificals, and proceeded to conduct a mock trial against it, swearing and blaspheming in an insane rage. The charges brought against the decaying corpse

were perjury, witchcraft, coveting the papacy, violating canon law, and anything else Stephen could think of. All Formosus's papal decrees were declared null and void.

The Pope had appointed a cardinal to answer on the corpse's behalf using an assumed voice, and so there was an element of farce to the grim proceedings as well. Not surprisingly, Formosus was found guilty. The corpse was stripped of its pontifical robes, and three fingers on its right hand (with which popes swore oaths and bestowed blessings) were sliced off. The cadaver was then buried in a common grave. Only a few days later, Stephen thought the better of it—he had the body exhumed again and thrown into the River Tiber. It was retrieved by a hermit and buried (for a third time) in an unmarked grave.

✝ ✝ ✝

Clearly, Stephen VI (VII) paid no attention to the beginning of the Papal Oath, which reads: "I vow to change nothing of the received Tradition, and nothing thereof I have found before me guarded by my God-pleasing predecessors, to encroach upon, to alter, or to permit any innovation therein."

✝ ✝ ✝

With all Formosus's ordinations now declared null, the clergy he had confirmed were required to submit letters to the pope

declaring their ordinations invalid and, in some cases, opening themselves to charges of heresy. The idea of the Cadaver Synod and the humiliation of the clerics outraged the Roman populace, who rioted against the pope in the hot summer of 897. Stephen was removed from office, imprisoned, and subsequently strangled.

It was during the brief twenty-day-reign of Theodore II that the decisions of the Cadaver Synod were overturned and Formosus was reinstated as pope. His body was exhumed once again and reburied in St. Peter's. In the subsequent reign of John IX, the Synod was finally denounced and the whole bizarre and grisly episode was consigned to Church history. And yet, echoes of the Cadaver Synod would reverberate for centuries, proving an embarrassment for the Church for many years to come.

NONEXISTENT POPES

From time to time, it has suited the Vatican to declare that there was someone sitting in St. Peter's throne when it was actually vacant. Why? Sometimes to prevent civil strife, sometimes to thwart a usurper, or sometimes to cover up administrative delays in the election of a pontiff following the death of his predecessor—but primarily to ensure a sense of continuity. A number of popes reigned for extremely short periods, leaving no record other than their name, and making it difficult to determine whether or not they ever existed. It seems clear, however, that others definitely did not.

Romanus (August–November 897)
Supreme pontiff of the universal church or a holding tactic?

In the upheavals that followed the Cadaver Synod, a.k.a. the *Synod Horrenda* (see page 55), Rome was split into a number of factions. When Stephen VI (VII), who was clearly mad and under the political control of the Duke of Spoleto, was deposed and killed, civil revolt threatened the Holy City. A pontiff named Romanus was hastily elected. Who was he, where did he come from, and *when* exactly was he elected? Some sources state that he was a deacon or bishop of San Pietro in Vincoli (St. Peter in

Chains) and that he had been made a cardinal by Stephen VI (VII); however, his name is unknown. If he *did* exist, he may have been a supporter of the exhumed Pope Formosus, who was hastily removed from office by an anti-Formosan faction.

This mystery pontiff issued no edicts and vacated Peter's seat after only two months. No one knows the date of his death, nor what became of him after his pontificate—although some have suggested he became a monk. Unusual for an allegedly Italian pope, he is *not* buried in St. Peter's.

It is possible that the Vatican simply used the name "Romanus" as a holding tactic to prevent revolution until a new pope could be elected. Scholars have noted the similarity between the pope's name and that of the Holy City itself. Romanus was succeeded by Theodore II, who reigned for only twenty days.

Lando (ca. August 913–ca. March 914)

A forgettable reign

Nobody can agree on whether or not Lando was consecrated as pope; likewise, nobody can agree on when he died, although allegedly there is a tomb in St. Peter's ascribed to him. Indeed, nobody can seem to agree on much at all in regard to his dubious reign. He is supposed to have ascended the papal throne

at a time when Rome was torn between very powerful Roman families, each intent on promoting their own interests through the papacy. The pontificate of his predecessor Anastasius III was completely dominated by the powerful Theophylact family and especially the ambitious Theodora, who was rumored to be the pope's mistress.

Rebellion was fomenting in Rome following Anastasius's ineffectual reign and the reign of his predecessor, the murderous Sergius III (see page 62). So, what happened? Perhaps one of two things:

1. With the throne empty, the Theophylact dynasty, with the backing of corrupt cardinals, pretended it was not in order to consolidate their position and overpower their rivals.

2. The Theophylacts placed an ordinary priest on the throne as a stopgap without ever making him pope.

Lando's six-month reign is utterly undistinguished. He issued no edicts—he may have had no authority—and there is no record of him officiating as pope outside of Rome. The only known record may be a donation, allegedly given in the memory of his father, to the cathedral-church in Sabina, possibly his place of birth. If Lando did reign, he was succeeded

by John X, who tried to challenge some of the powerful and corrupt families of Rome—he was imprisoned and suffocated to death for his trouble.

John XX

The pope that never was

During the tenth and eleventh centuries, the name John was one of the most popular—and unlucky—papal choices. The frequency of the name created confusion in the medieval Vatican records, so that when Petrus Hispanus (Peter of Spain—the only Portuguese man and the only doctor to serve as pope) was elected in September 1276, officials insisted that he take the name John XXI, even though there hadn't been a John XX. Was this to rectify some discrepancy in earlier records? No one knows for sure. The name "John XX" does appear in some religious rolls, but no dates are given for him, since apparently he never existed.

MURDEROUS POPE

Sergius III (January 29, 904–April 14, 911)

While Sergius II (see page 47) is thought to have been closely associated with criminals and assassins, he was nowhere near as vicious as one of his successors, the murderous Sergius III. The brutality began during his ascendancy. His predecessor, the unfortunate Leo V, had been overthrown, kidnapped, and imprisoned by an antipope named Christopher. Acting on the instructions of a Lateran convention, Sergius (then bishop of Caere) overthrew Christopher but did not release Leo, as he had been told to do. Instead, he threw the two men into the same cell and declared himself pope. He would later arrange for both Leo and Christopher to be strangled, one surefire way to avoid a challenge to his reign.

Sergius dated his reign from 897, when he had been first "elected," and quickly settled in to take revenge on his enemies. Gripped by a hatred of Formosus, Sergius forced the clergy to nullify all the edicts of John IX—which had been formally ratified by two synods, one in Rome and one in Ravenna—and to reinstate all the findings of the Cadaver Synod, which were at this point considered heretical. All clergy who had been consecrated by either John or Formosus were stripped of their office and subjected to humiliation. All those who had been ordained

⚷ DID SERGIUS III DESERVE THE PAPACY? ⚷

There was *some* validity in Sergius's claim to the papacy. He had been consecrated as bishop by Pope Formosus (see "The Exhumed Pope," page 55) and had actually been part of the Cadaver Synod under Stephen VI (VII). He had been chosen to succeed Theodore II in 897, but was quickly ejected and driven into exile by a pro-Formosan faction that elected John IX, with the support of the powerful Lambert of Spoleto. The ousting had always rankled Sergius, who had resolved to seize the papacy for himself at the earliest opportunity.

since Formosus were forced to take their ordinations again; the pope could personally object to any one of them, which he did on several occasions.

✝✝✝

"[T]he Roman pontiff, by reason of his office as Vicar of Christ, and as pastor of the entire Church, has full, supreme, and universal power over the whole Church, a power which he can always exercise unhindered."

—*Lumen Gentium* (Dogmatic Constitution on the Church)

✝✝✝

Such moves were illegal, as far as the Church was concerned, but Sergius had the support of some of the most important Roman families (such as the Theophylacts, who controlled a powerful

militia) and few dared challenge him. Sergius had no reservations about ordering the deaths or "disappearances" of those who spoke out against him.

✝✝✝

The pope's friendship with the Theophylact family did not stop him from raping their fifteen-year-old daughter Theodora and leaving her with child. The infant would become the future Pope John XI, the only recorded successor to the papacy of illegitimate birth.

✝✝✝

Like Sergius II before him, Sergius III quickly made connections with the criminal underworld in Rome. Soon he was running most of the gambling rackets, prostitution, and "coining" (forgery) within the city. He was also suspected of being behind a spate of burglaries and killings that swept the city during his reign but, as he was pope, nobody could prove him guilty. His big moneymaker was the sale of "indulgences," or forgivenesses.

✝✝✝

Any sin, no matter how heinous, could be forgiven by the pope (who was not above badly sinning himself) as long as the offender had enough money to pay for that forgiveness. Such absolutions could even be given in advance. This allowed the wealthy to sin with impunity while the pope fattened his pockets.

✝✝✝

Not content with his schemes in Rome, Sergius threw the Eastern Church into disarray by condoning the fourth marriage of Byzantine Emperor Leo IV in the furtherance of seeking an heir. Since Leo's third wife was still alive, this was in defiance of Eastern Canonical Law and roundly condemned by the Byzantine Church, which appealed to the pope for support. Leo, however, was prepared to pay a hefty sum for papal approval, which was duly forthcoming. For an additional sum, Sergius deposed, excommunicated, and drove into exile the Patriarch of Constantinople, who had been one of the Emperor's strongest critics.

✂ THE WORST OF THE PORNOCRACY ✂

So corrupt and licentious were Sergius and his successors that their collective reigns were referred to as "the pornocracy" and are regarded among the most scandalous eras for the papacy. Sergius, however, stood out as one of the most vicious of them all. From the papal throne, he blithely ordered stabbings, poisonings, and strangulations with neither compunction nor hesitation. Those lesser criminals who dared to compete against him were usually arrested on some trumped-up minor charge and removed to the Vatican dungeons where they could be tortured and killed on the papal whim.

Sergius then set about restoring the Lateran Basilica, part of which had been destroyed by the earthquake that occurred during the Cadaver Synod. Supporters of the exhumed Pope Formosus took this as a sign of God's displeasure at the Synod, but Sergius said that God wished the Lateran to be developed in his (Sergius's) image. This, of course, was blasphemy—but presumably the pope had already granted himself absolution.

THE STEADY MARCH OF PROTESTANTISM

The conduct of certain popes contributed greatly to the gradual but relentless rise of Protestantism in Western Europe. As early as the thirteenth and fourteenth centuries, mainstream churchmen began to question papal behavior for obvious reasons; there had been many disgraceful moments in the history of the papacy that compromised public opinion. For example, during the Great Western Schism (1378–1417) (see page 151) a plethora of popes denounced and excommunicated one another, weakening perception of the papacy and, more importantly, the authority of the Church. Additionally, church-goers had every reason to question the sanctity of the Vicars of Christ when confronted with the licentious actions of John XII (955–964), the criminal connections of Sergius II (844–847), the worldliness of Innocent VIII (1484–1492) and Clement VI (1342–1352), and when they saw the papacy actually sold by Benedict IX (1032–1048).

† † †

Is it really possible that Celestine V (1294)—who never washed, and sat in his own ordure—or a ranting psychopath such as Urban VI (1378–1389), or indeed an incredibly frail

pontiff such as Clement XII (1730–1740) were really the embodiments of Christ himself?

✝ ✝ ✝

Furthermore, given that the papacy owned much territory and was quite wealthy, it was temping for those who had been elected to behave in a manner better suited to an earthly ruler than a saintly Church leader. They forged alliances with kings and manipulated political situations for their own advantage—and several popes, in turn, were manipulated by other monarchs.

No wonder why more spiritually minded thinkers expressed dismay and even outright anger at the popes' corrupt behavior. One of those who condemned the Church for its lack of moral authority was Dutchman Desiderius Erasmus of Rotterdam (1466–1536).

The theologian was especially critical of Julius II (1503–1513), known as "the warrior pope," who had put on armor and led an army to seize the city of Mirandola in January 1511. Erasmus found the pope's focus on military and political aspects of the world to be distasteful. The Dutchman also drew attention to one of Julius's predecessors, Alexander VI (1492–1503), whose papal reign had been full of political maneuvering, chicanery, and debauchery. This was no way for a pontiff to behave, Erasmus thought. In 1511,

he penned a work entitled *In Praise of Folly,* which mocked and satirized the Church, its pope, and his machinery of government—and he caustically dedicated it to Julius II. This, together with Erasmus's other work, *Colloquia* (published in 1519), laid the very foundations for later ideological rebellions against the pontiffs that would gradually lead to the Protestant Revolution.

Erasmus was not the first to criticize Church abuses and the behavior of the popes. Earlier critics included the English theologian John Wycliffe (ca. 1320–1384), who had translated the Bible into English between the years 1382 and 1395.

✂ ERASMUS ✂

Illegitimate by birth, Erasmus was born to a priest and the daughter of a Rotterdam physician. Despite these unusual circumstances, he was cared for by both parents until they died from the plague in 1483. Although his given name was Gerard Gerardson, he later took the name Erasmus after a saint and also from the Greek *Erasmios* meaning "beloved." Erasmus grew up to be a renowned thinker, lecturer, and theologian, having studied and taught at Oxford University in England.

✝ ✝ ✝

Up to the fourteenth century, the Bible was written in Latin, the language of the Catholic Church and especially of the Roman pontificate. The Old Testament had originally been

written in Hebrew, and the New Testament, in Greek, though a few portions of each were written in Aramaic.

✝ ✝ ✝

It was a daring, unauthorized move, and it inspired the Lollard movement, a group of Wycliffe's followers who were critical of Church procedures and the pontificate. Wycliffe's teachings also influenced others, such as the Bohemian martyr John Huss (ca. 1369–July 6, 1415), who was burned at the stake after being excommunicated and declared a heretic by Pope (now antipope) Alexander V.

✝ ✝ ✝

Erasmus, Wycliffe, and other reformers of the time were aided by an important technological advance altering much of Western Europe—the printing press. Prior to this invention, ideas had been conveyed by word of mouth or by letters; now they could be printed and circulated to a much wider audience.

✝ ✝ ✝

Possibly one of the most influential of all the reformers was a German Augustinian monk named Martin Luther (1483–1546), who had read Erasmus and Wycliffe and was intrigued by their thinking. He, too, was dismayed by the excesses of the papacy,

particularly since he lived in the era of worldly Renaissance popes. But it was the excessively worldly pontificate of Leo X (1513–1521) and the Dominican preacher Johann Tezel's selling of papal indulgences that ultimately triggered Luther's rebellion. He nailed his "Ninety-Five Theses" against the church door at Wittenberg Cathedral.

✝ ✝ ✝

The Cathedral was rumored to hold a hair from the head of the Virgin that would excuse any sin of a man who looked upon it (and made a substantial payment to Rome) for 999 years.

✝ ✝ ✝

Luther's views took about a year to reach Leo, who condemned him and instructed the general of his order to rein him in. Following a series of debates between Luther and the Catholic theologian John Eck in Leipzig, Germany, Leo was forced to issue a papal bull, *Exsurge Dominae*, in June 1520, virulently condemning Luther on forty-one items. Luther showed his contempt for the pope's utterances by publicly burning the bull on December 10, 1520. Leo then excommunicated him in a further bull, *Decet Romanum Pontificem*, issued on January 3, 1521. But that was not the end of the story.

On January 22, 1521, Holy Roman Emperor Charles V summoned an assembly in the German town of Worms on the River

Rhine. He commanded Luther to appear to give an account of his teaching. And Luther did, offering a spirited and carefully thought-out defense of his position. Although the resulting *Edict of Worms* roundly condemned his writings and teachings and forbade it within Western Christendom, the Emperor had miscalculated; the Diet of Worms had actually given the rebel monk a platform for his views and raised his profile among those dissatisfied with the Roman Church. Luther's carefully reasoned arguments continued to draw more and more people toward the Protestant ideal.

The papacy had failed to recognize both the nature and strength of the rebellion within the Church. Nor had it grasped the urgent need to root out corruption and abuse within its own structure. Leo continued to live in the style of a monarchical pope, largely ignoring the problems that were building up around him. Then, with the crisis seriously deepening, he died on December 1, 1522, bequeathing the situation to his successor Adrian V (1522–1523).

Adrian's handling of the matter was singularly inept. The beginning of his reign coincided with the fall of Rhodes to the Turks, and Adrian turned his attention from the growing tide of Protestantism to call for a crusade. Because the pope had managed to alienate the two most powerful figures on

the European stage, Charles V (the Holy Roman Emperor) and Francis I of France, his call was barely heeded. He was forced to enter a humiliating alliance with several cities and countries in order to protect himself—evidence of the pope's ineffectiveness in the eyes of his enemies. As far as Protestantism was concerned, he rounded on the Curia, blaming them (and not the papacy) for the Church's woes and thus alienating his cardinals. ✦ Curia: the administrative apparatus of the Holy See; similar in some respects to a government. ✦ With neither political nor Church backing, he cut a very lonely figure and was reviled by Protestant leaders. Come September 1523, Adrian was worn out by his exertions, crushed by his humiliations, and exhausted by the Roman heat (he was Dutch); he fell seriously ill and died that month.

✝ ✝ ✝

Adrian was initially buried in the chapel of San Andrea in St. Peter's, between the tombs of Pius II and Pius III. A Roman wit later added graffiti to his grave: "*Hic jacet impius inter Pios*" (here lies an impious between two Piuses).

✝ ✝ ✝

Adrian's successor, Clement VII (1523–1534), of the Medici family, was more concerned with preserving his family's hold on Florence and the papacy's hold on the Papal States than in

halting the spread of Protestantism. He failed to deal with the spread of the Protestant faith in Scandinavia and Switzerland and did not lend support to reform movements within the Church, which might have hindered the coming revolution. It was down to *his* successor, Paul III (1534–1549), to formulate some sort of response to the turning tide. It was he who convened the Council of Trent (December 13, 1545–December 4, 1563), and therefore launched what became known as the Catholic Counter-Revolution. Nevertheless, Paul was a Renaissance pope in every sense of the word—he staged banquets and masked balls, he hunted, and he was a patron of the arts. His administration was riddled with nepotism. In an attempt to prove his spirituality and high moral standards, he censured the artist Michelangelo for the nudity in some of his creations. The artist responded with a picture of the pope sporting donkey ears, much to the glee of Protestant reformers.

The latter part of Paul III's reign was dominated by family disputes between his son Pierluigi and Holy Roman Emperor Charles V. His successor, Julius III, was obsessed with a young boy; and *his* successor, Marcellus II, although promising much, reigned for only twenty-one days. It was Paul IV (1555–1559) who finally tried to get a grip on the situation, but he was so

authoritarian and deeply unpopular that his strict reforms alienated many believers. By then it was far too late anyway.

At this point, radical reformers such as John Calvin had come to the fore in places like Geneva, making the question of papal authority a central plank of their teaching. Calvin and his followers were not slow in condemning the papacy and Church structures, and by the time Pius IV (1559–1565) reconvened the Council of Trent—which had actually been in abeyance for almost ten years—Protestantism had become deeply entrenched and the situation was almost beyond saving. The rejection of the papacy had become one of the main strands of the new dispensation, and the popes found themselves branded as "the Antichrist" and the "Whore of Babylon" in radical Protestant teaching, some of which has continued to the present day. In a sense, the papacy was to some extent its own worst

> ### ✂ THE COUNCIL OF TRENT ✂
>
> **Paul III assembled the Council of Trent to condemn Luther's teaching and the spread of Protestantism, as well as to reaffirm and promulgate Catholic values and doctrine. Although seen as the first blow in the Counter-Revolution, it had something of a stuttering existence, mainly due to the temperament of the pope.**

enemy. The behavior and style of certain popes, and their initially lethargic response to the criticism leveled at them, allowed Protestantism to take a firm hold on the European mind. The lives of the popes themselves often provided a focus for dissent. By the time the seventeenth century dawned, the reformed faith was a fact of life.

PROMISCUOUS POPE

John XII (December 16, 955–May 14, 964)

Although a number of popes can certainly be classed as "promiscuous," few match John XII in the realms of sexual excess. Elected at the age of eighteen thanks to his father, Alberic II—who was, in effect, absolute ruler of Rome at the time—John became pontiff amid great celebration.

✝ ✝ ✝

John was originally named Octavian, and only the third pope in history to change his name.

✝ ✝ ✝

There was said to be no sexual act or perversion that the pope would not try, and he not only consorted openly with "the whores of Rome" but also with young boys and animals. All this was carried out within the Vatican precincts and it became a major scandal throughout Rome. Seeing the damage that the pope's behavior was doing to the Church, the cardinals called upon him to amend his ways. John ignored the rebukes made against him and continued to indulge his extreme sexual fantasies. The clergy threatened to remove him—unabashedly, he told them to do so. He was the pope, after all, and had the support of the Roman people.

Despite all this hedonistic activity and blatant disregard for spiritual matters, John did find time to engage on a few subjects concerning the Church. He issued counsel to representatives of the Spanish Church, which was under repeated Moorish attacks and sought the pope's guidance. He appears to have been extremely drunk at the time, however, so the advice went unrecorded. He presented the pallium to the visiting archbishops of York and Canterbury and made several pilgrimages to the monastery of Subiaco, fifty miles east of Rome, in which his father had taken an interest. On the political front, he engaged in a disastrous campaign to extend the papal lands by trying to annex the areas of Capua and Benevento, a region that at the time was being plundered by the King of Italy. John's plan was blocked by the Italian sovereign, who threatened to march on Rome. In response, John dispatched emissaries to the German court of Otto to ask for his military aid in exchange for an imperial crown. Otto accepted and was duly crowned the Holy Roman Emperor (the first ever), but the

promised aid was not forthcoming and the pope's military expedition foundered.

Still, it was the pope's sexual escapades that attracted the most attention and eventually turned the Church against him. During a papal procession for the Feast of Easter, a young boy caught the eye of the extremely drunken pope. Breaking from the procession, the pontiff pursued him through the streets, hoisting up his robes as he ran. Shortly thereafter he was caught "in a lewd act" with the quivering child in an alley.

A 963 synod deposed John and, fearful of a German invasion in his support, asked the German Emperor Otto to propose a successor whom the cardinals would then elect. Otto proposed a layman named Leo, who took the name Leo VIII and was duly confirmed on December 4, 963. An arrogant and resentful John declared the synod's decision totally invalid on two counts—it had not been properly convened with the authority to depose a sitting pope and it had consulted a German Emperor to decide the papal succession.

Back in Rome, Leo was not popular. He had passed several unwelcome edicts and, like John, the Roman people questioned German involvement in the election of a Roman pope. Many sided with John, who continued to stir up resentment against

Leo with intimidation tactics and bribes. Rome simmered on the edge of outright revolt, and, with the German Emperor and his troops now departed, it seemed extremely likely.

In February 964, yet another synod was convened to overturn the decisions of the previous one and to reinstate John as pope. Leo VIII was deposed and all his edicts were declared invalid. John returned to the city in great triumph, but once back in the Vatican, his bawdy antics continued unabated. Rumors swirled that elderly and married women, as well as small boys, were constantly entering and leaving the pope's chambers. With the reputation of the Holy Office in serious danger, the cardinals once again called on the pope to mend his ways; and once again John paid them no heed.

Plus, another threat was looming. The deposed Pope Leo had gone to Germany seeking aid from his sponsor Otto. The German Emperor acted in Leo's favor, marching on Rome once more. John fled, however, knowing that Otto had interests elsewhere and couldn't afford to mount a continuous presence in Rome. When the Germans withdrew, John returned, promptly declaring Leo a heretic and excommunicating him.

At the end of April 964, the cardinals met again to consider the continuing German threat and also to discuss the future of the papacy. John made it clear that any of their decisions

regarding his conduct would be ignored. At the beginning of May, he suffered a severe stroke and died of a subsequent heart attack a week later.

John had reigned a little over ten years and was only twenty-eight when he died.

The position of pope was reoffered to Leo VIII, but by now the Holy Office was so mired in sleaze, controversy, and outright filth that he refused it (and as Otto's initial appointment, he would not have been accepted by the Roman people anyway). Instead, one of the cardinal-deacons was elected to popular acclaim—Benedict V. He reigned for exactly one month (see "The Two Popes," page 82).

"TWO POPES" X 2

On a number of occasions, there have been multiple popes ruling simultaneously—during the Great Western Schism, for example— but at least they usually had the good sense to be in different places. In the curious reigns of Leo VIII and Benedict V, both claimants to the papacy were in Rome, playing musical chairs with St. Peter's chair. In the case of Benedict VI and Boniface VII the two had a vicious rivalry that ended in death.

Leo VIII (December 6, 963–March 1, 965) and Benedict V (May 22–June 23, 964)
The instant pope and the invisible pope

The problems began with the licentious Pope John XII (see "The Promiscuous Pope," page 77), who was deposed on December 4 by order of a synod under the leadership of the German Emperor Otto. John refused to accept the decision but nevertheless fled to Tivoli, where he continued to fulminate against the synod that had deposed him. In the meantime, the chair of St. Peter lay vacant.

With no obvious candidate to succeed him and with the papacy mired in controversy, the Church was faced with a problem. There was one possibility, a skilled Lateran official

who had a good reputation and who had carried on fairly well during the profligacy of the previous pope. However, he was a layman and held no Church rank. This did not stop him from being elected as Leo VIII, with Emperor Otto's approval and great acclaim throughout the Church. However, Leo's candidacy had to be rushed through: almost in a matter of days, he was consecrated into the Church, hurried through minor and major orders, and formally elected as pope.

✝✝✝

The whole thing was done with unseemly and almost farcical haste—in the morning, Leo was a priest, in the afternoon a cardinal, and pope the next day.

✝✝✝

Predictably, the deposed John denounced the new pontiff from his refuge in Tivoli and sought to excommunicate him. *He* was still the true pope, John claimed, casting doubts on the legitimacy of his deposition. Curiously, the *Annuario Pontificio* records the overlap of papal reigns without comment or explanation.

As soon as Otto and his troops left Rome, John began to stir up unrest in the city. In retaliation, Leo denounced the former pope (who still enjoyed some support) and began to tax a number of businesses in order to raise funds for the Vatican

coffers, which John had all but depleted. As the riots grew worse, Leo was forced to flee the city and take refuge at the imperial German court, allowing John to reenter the city and declare himself pope once more. A second synod convened, deposed Leo as a usurper, and declared his ordination, consecration, and edicts invalid.

After he regained the papal throne, in 964 John XII suddenly suffered a stroke—supposedly in the bed of a married woman—and died soon after. Leo returned to Rome and was half-heartedly offered the papacy once again; by this time, the office was so caught up in scandal that he refused. In any case, the cardinals showed more interest in the cardinal-deacon Benedict, whom they elected in May 964 as Benedict V. Although he was certainly a churchman, his election was just as dubious as Leo's had been, and it is doubtful that he was even elected by formal vote.

Leo then flip-flopped, deciding that he wanted the seat after all. He denounced Benedict, called his election illegitimate (nevermind his own spurious rise to power), and urged him to stand down as pontiff. When Benedict refused, Leo called upon his old ally, the German emperor Otto, for assistance. Otto called on the Roman people to reinstate Leo; when they did not,

he marched on the city, laying siege and threatening to starve the inhabitants into submission. On June 23, the city surrendered and Otto and Leo both entered. A synod was convened and presided over by both Leo and Otto—thus, its conclusions were hardly surprising. Benedict was condemned once more as a usurper and literally stripped of the papacy—his pontifical vestments and insignia were removed, and he was forced to lie prostrate while his pontifical crosier was broken above his head by Leo himself. ✦ Crosier: the stylized staff of a leading cleric, representing pastoral office. ✦ Otto now effectively controlled the papacy but allowed Benedict to remain in the rank of deacon in Hamburg. Still widely admired in the Church for his holiness and intellect, Benedict was reoffered the papacy when Leo VIII died only one year later. Benedict returned to Rome and was restored to the papal throne, where he was largely ignored by political leaders. After only a matter of weeks, he gave up the papacy and returned to Hamburg, where he died in July 966.

✝✝✝

Benedict's body, originally buried in German soil, was returned to Rome by the German emperor Otto III; the exact location of his grave remains unknown.

✝✝✝

Benedict VI (January 19, 973–June 974) and Boniface VII (May 973–July 20, 985)

Rival Popes

With the Church in turmoil and largely in thrall to the German Emperor, Benedict VI ascended to the papal throne in January 973. Like his predecessor, he was a creature of Otto I and the circumstances surrounding his election remain obscure. What *is* known is that he had to wait until the Emperor returned to Rome to give his approval before he could be consecrated. The delay angered reformers, who resented political intervention in the process.

But, there was another problem: one of the most powerful, wealthy, and corrupt families in Rome, the Crescentiis, had set their eyes on the papacy. They had allied themselves with the reformist cardinals and a nationalist movement that was opposed to Benedict's election. They had picked another candidate to succeed John XIII, a cardinal-deacon named Franco who was in the pay of the Crescentiis—but Benedict was Otto's man and he had been elected. Using a mixture of bribery and promises among the cardinals, the Crescentiis went ahead anyway; several days after Benedict was consecrated, Franco was made a rival pope, taking the name Boniface VII. Benedict promptly

denounced him and called on Otto to enforce his decision. However, by then the German emperor had returned to the imperial court and fallen ill. On May 7, 974, he died. His son Otto II was preoccupied with troubles in Germany and could spare no troops to help Benedict.

The Crescentiis saw their chance and, under cover of a popular revolt that they themselves had stirred, seized the pope and imprisoned him in Castel Sant'Angelo. Otto II promptly dispatched a representative to demand Benedict's release; but, hearing that he was coming, Boniface quickly ordered that Benedict be strangled.

✝ ✝ ✝

Some accounts say that Boniface choked his opponent with his bare hands; others say the murder was carried out by a priest named Stephen acting on Boniface's direct orders.

✝ ✝ ✝

The imperial representative arrived with a German force, outraged by the murder. Boniface fled, taking a portion of the papal treasury with him. Another pope was hastily elected, taking the name Benedict VII, and Boniface was excommunicated. However, he returned to Rome six years later, as Otto II lay ill and dying, to reclaim the papacy from the unpopular Benedict VII.

With popular support—bought for him by the Crescentiis—he had Benedict deposed, imprisoned, and murdered. He then assumed St. Peter's chair.

✂ WAS BONIIFACE VII LEGITMATE OR NOT? ✂

Despite his wicked ways and the circumstances of his election, Boniface VII was considered a legitimate pope until 1904; the next pope to assume the name numbered himself Boniface VIII. On the orders of Pius X (1903–1914), however, he was declared an antipope and his name was stricken from records. However, in some Vatican records, his pontificate is still presented as legitimate, dated from the death of John XIV. In others, he is not mentioned at all; and in still others, he is classified as an antipope during the reigns of Benedict VII or John XIV.

Boniface VII continued to rule for another eleven months without opposition from the Church. However, the ailing Otto, stricken with malaria, began making threatening demands that the cardinals appoint another pope. Fearing an attack by German armies, Boniface fled to Constantinople. The cardinals, obeying Otto's request and also fearful that Rome would be attacked, elected Peter Campanora of Pavia, who took the name John XIV (December 983–August 20, 984).

Despite his dire health, Otto traveled to Rome to see and approve the new pope's consecration, but the journey proved too much for him and he died in the pontiff's arms. Hearing that Otto was dead, Boniface returned from Constantinople and, with popular backing, seized the throne once more. He had John imprisoned, beaten, and poisoned. Less than a year later, Boniface himself was dead—some accounts state that he, too, may have been poisoned. His body was stripped of its vestments, dragged naked through the Roman streets, and left at the foot of Marcus Aurelius's statue (then in front of the Lateran Palace), where it was trampled upon and repeatedly prodded with spears and swords, as small pieces of his anatomy were cut off. He was from then on referred to as "Malefatius" (evil doer) rather than "Bonifatus" (doer of good).

"THREE TIMES" POPE

Benedict IX (October 21, 1032–September 1044; March–May 1045; November 8, 1047–July 16, 1048)

Only one man has the distinction of holding the papacy on three separate occasions.

Benedict was the son of his predecessor, John XIX, and a Theophylact, the powerful family that had supplied pontiffs for well over a generation. His election was manifestly arranged through bribery, since Benedict was only fourteen at the time and had not held any prior Church office. As soon as he became pope, he did four things:

1. He handed out favors to members of his family.
2. He took a mistress.
3. He placed several abbeys under direct papal protection—meaning he could loot their treasures and claim he was taking them into custody to safeguard them from robbers.
4. He took several more mistresses.

Needless to say, the pope's conduct was becoming scandalous, and the clergy wasn't happy.

However, it was not the clerics but the Roman people who took action by rioting and threatening to march on the Vatican

and the Lateran Palace, where the pope had installed one of his mistresses. Alarmed by this turn of events, Benedict fled, planning to return once the dust had settled. However, the riots continued, keeping the pope away for some time.

Although Benedict had never formally been deposed, the rival Crescentii family elected a papal nominee of their own—John, bishop of Sabina. He took the name Sylvester III. The election was enough to tip the balance in Benedict's favor: the Roman people might not have *liked* him, but they did believe he'd been anointed by God. The now-married Benedict seized his chance. He excommunicated Sylvester, cobbled together an army, and marched on Rome. The people grudgingly offered him St. Peter's chair once again.

Back in Rome, Benedict divorced his wife and took a mistress, but within two months he was bored with the papacy. He decided to quit (at a price) and remarry the woman he'd just divorced. Benedict offered to sell the papacy to his grandfather, John Gratian, who took the throne without election as Gregory VI.

The new pope now faced Sylvester III. Each declared the other a heretic and ordered excommunications. Just to complicate matters, the ever-fickle Benedict decided that he wanted to buy back the papacy and resume his pontifical duties . . . and

indiscretions. When Gregory refused, Benedict excommunicated both his rival claimants on the grounds that he was the only properly elected pontiff.

With the papacy looking like a farce, the German Emperor Henry III took up the issue. In 1046, he came to Italy to be crowned and was greeted with what looked like a circus. In utter frustration, he summoned all three claimants to a synod at Sutri. At first, Benedict refused to attend—he had retreated to his family estates outside Rome with a large retinue of prostitutes and drunkards to "ease him through a difficult time." But when Henry threatened to invade papal lands, Benedict reluctantly agreed. In the meantime, the Synod of Sutri deposed both Sylvester and Gregory; four days later, on Christmas Eve 1046, they finally deposed Benedict as well. They then moved to elect Suidger of Bamburg as pope, and he took the name Clement II. Benedict, however, refused to recognize the new pope, claiming that his election was invalid due to a politically motivated synod under control of the German Emperor. He consequently excommunicated Clement and declared himself pope once more. When Henry again threatened invasion, Benedict withdrew to his estates and left Rome to its new pope.

Clement's reign lasted only eight months in total. Then he suddenly and inexplicably died—although some say he was

poisoned. With St. Peter's chair vacant, Benedict declared himself pope yet again, and the Roman people, who had no doubt received bribes and promises from both him and his family, supported him. They demanded his return, and in November 1047, Benedict entered the city as Vicar of Christ.

The despondent Emperor Henry chose a German, Poppo of Brixen, for the papacy, and threatened to attack Rome if the population did not agree. When the Roman citizenry acknowledged the German pope, renamed Damasus II, Benedict was forced to flee to his Tusculan estates. There, surrounded by mistresses and prostitutes, he continued to act as pope, issuing edicts and excommunicating Damasus and his successor Leo IX. But nobody paid him much attention.

In April 1049, he was summoned to appear before a Lateran council on a charge of simony, but refused to do so and was duly excommunicated. ✦ Simony: the buying and selling of spiritual goods and church offices. ✦ In return, he promptly excommunicated every member of the council that had summoned him—but such edicts were completely invalid. He would live for another seven years, fulminating against the Roman papacy, and would be buried not in St. Peter's but in the abbey church of Grottaferrata in the Alban Hills.

THE EASTERN SCHISM (1054)

The origins of the Eastern Schism have usually been rather grandiosely ascribed to theological differences, but they had more to do with political, linguistic, and geographic issues. And, although the date of the Schism is given as 1054, during the reign of Pope Leo IX, a serious divide between the two churches had been emerging long before that.

The East-West Schism was the first serious split to rock Chalcedonian Christianity in the medieval period. Most of the churches of the West might be described as "Chalcedonian," in that they follow the dictates of the Council of Chalcedon (AD 451), which ruled on the nature of Jesus. The Council held that he was composed of two elements—both human and divine—and that it was only through him that humans could know God. This thinking was accepted by most of the churches of the West and even by the Protestant Church when they emerged in the sixteenth century. The Eastern Church had a slightly different perspective. Tensions rose to the surface with the insertion of the "filioque clause" in the Nicene Creed, which gave Jesus equal status to God. ✦ Filoque: a word from the Latin root meaning "and the son." ✦ That one move is blamed for causing the theological split between the two branches of the Church.

The creed, the bedrock of Western Christendom, had been hammered out at the Council of Nicea in 325. In its original form it stated, "We believe in the Holy Spirit—who proceeds from the Father . . ." However, in 381 some thinkers inserted the filioque clause, which amended the text to "We believe in the Holy Spirit—who proceeds from the Father and the Son," thus asserting the divinity of Jesus. This amendment was accepted unquestioningly in the West, but not in the East. Indeed, Pope Leo III (792–816) came under pressure from the Frankish Emperor Charlemagne to declare it an important part of church worship. While Leo resisted the Emperor's urgings for fear of alienating the Eastern Church, he did not exactly forbid its use. However, at Charlemagne's prompting, he did condemn the frequent use of icons that were a feature of Eastern worship.

While the pope, as Bishop of Rome, was quietly accepting the filioque, the great patriarchs of the East—the bishops of Antioch, Constantinople, and Jerusalem—were vehemently denouncing it. All four bishops had been confirmed as equals by the Council of Chalcedon, but now the Roman pope was trying to exert his superiority.

The growing antipathy came to a head in the eleventh century. Leo IX, the third pope imposed on the Church by the

German Emperor Henry III, decided to unify papal lands in the south of Italy following a number of incursions by the Normans. In the course of Leo's disastrous campaign, his troops over-ran an area of southern Italy claimed by Byzantium, known as the Italian Catepanate. The anti-Latin Patriarch of Constantinople, Michael Cerularius, used the opportunity to denounce the Roman pontiffs, and especially Leo, who had been captured during the south Italian campaign and was being held prisoner. The Patriarch closed down all Latin churches in Constantinople and expelled Humbert, the archbishop of Sicily, from the areas claimed by Byzantium. He further denounced all Rome's practices and forbade his followers to accept any Eucharist made from unleavened bread.

✂ A GROWING SPLIT ✂

	Roman Church	Eastern Church
Official language	Latin	Greek
Eucharist	Unleavened bread permitted	Unleavened bread considered anti-Scriptural
Sex Lives	Vow of celibacy for priests	Allowed clergy to marry

Although still a prisoner, Leo IX sent a delegation led by Humbert to Constantinople. The mission was a spectacular failure, as both sides were utterly unyielding. On July 6, 1054, in front of the entire congregation of the Hagia Sophia (the Church of Holy Wisdom in what is now Istanbul), Humbert placed a papal bull on the altar, officially excommunicating the Patriarch and his followers. Michael Cerularius responded with his own condemnations and expulsions just over two weeks later. When released from prison after making humiliating concessions to his captors, Leo IX continued his condemnation of the Eastern Church and the patriarchs. However, he was worn out by his period in captivity and took seriously ill, dying shortly afterward with the situation still unresolved. The schism deepened as Eastern patriarchs still refused to recognize the authority of the Bishop of Rome.

During the reign of Gregory X (1272–1276), an attempt was made to reconcile the two branches of the Church. The pope invited and made overtures toward representatives of the Eastern Church at the Second Council of Lyons, which opened on May 7, 1274. However, his main purpose was *not* restoring Christian union; rather, he hoped to secure funding from the East for a crusade that would secure the holy lands of the Middle

East from Saracen domination. In the end, the crusade never took place and the Schism remained. It remains in place today, nearly a thousand years later, with no resolution in sight—a testament to the intransigence of both factions of the Church.

USURPER POPE

Honorius II (December 21, 1124–February 13, 1130)

There are few more indecent moments in Church history than the election of Honorius II to papal office. On the death of his predecessor Callistus II, a powerful Roman faction headed by the wealthy Pierleoni family saw an opportunity to increase their influence and status in the city. Bribing a substantial number of cardinals, they threw their weight behind Cardinal Saxo of the church of San Stephano. Saxo proved difficult, demanding money and favors if he stood as pope, and the Pierleonis quickly abandoned him in favor of an elderly cardinal-priest named Teobaldo, whom they elected on December 15, 1124, and who took the name Celestine II. The move was not a popular one with other elements in the coalition, particularly the equally powerful Frangipani family who, also having abandoned Saxo, had decided on their own candidate, Lamberto, cardinal-bishop of Ostia. Thinking that Teobaldo was too close to the Pierleonis, they convened a synod of their own and, by bribing a different set of cardinals, elected Lamberto as pope.

As Celestine was being formally consecrated as pope, the Frangipanis made their move. With the secret support of Aimeric, the Chancellor of the Holy Roman Church, they broke into the

sacred ceremony and, with much violence, proclaimed Lamberto as pope. Celestine suffered a number of serious wounds in the attack and offered to resign. A heated debate broke out as to whether or not the old man had been consecrated, and Pierleoni supporters pointed out that with such grievous injuries he would not rule for long and should be allowed to continue. Lamberto, however, had other ideas. Drawing his sword, he threatened the priests all around, and they conducted the ceremony with swords at their throats. Thus, Lamberto was installed as pope after what was deemed a "reelection," and he took the name Honorius II.

✝ ✝ ✝

Honorius was a surprising choice for a name since it had been largely discredited by Honorius I, who was formally condemned by the Third Council of Constantinople in 680 for supporting Monothelitism (in essence, denying the humanity of Christ). However, two other popes would use the name as well.

✝ ✝ ✝

His first act as pope was to declare the coronation of Celestine II invalid—the old pope had neither been consecrated nor enthroned—and to banish the wounded, old man from Rome.

As a pope, Honorius was reasonably capable. Much of his pontificate was concerned with carrying through the reforms

that had been hammered out by his predecessor Callistus II and the German Emperor Henry V. He relied heavily on the Chancellor Aimeric, who was now one of the most powerful men in the Holy See. Although Honorius was certainly not a puppet of the Frangipanis, he did work closely with them, leading to many allegations, especially regarding the allocation of benefices. There also seems little doubt that the Pierleonis were stirring up the Roman populace against the pope, declaring that he had usurped the papacy from their candidate Celestine.

In January 1130, Honorius suddenly fell ill. Aimeric immediately removed him from Rome, where hostility toward him may have been growing, and had him taken to the monastery of San Gregorio in the Caelian Hills, which was protected by the Frangipani family. Shortly after arriving there, Honorius died. So unpopular was he by now that Aimeric had him temporarily buried in the monastery grounds until his successor, Innocent II, was elected and the body could be safely returned to Rome for a formal burial in the Lateran.

JEWISH POPE

Anacletus II (February 23, 1130–January 25, 1138)

"Is the pope a Catholic?" Well, not always. In some instances, he may not even have been Christian. The first pope, St. Peter, was of course Jewish—but he was not the only one.

Anacletus was born Pietro Pierleoni into a prominent wealthy Christian family that had converted from Judaism. In a highly divisive election, he was chosen by a majority of the cardinals, though not all.

Those opposed to Anacletus withdrew and planned to elect another pope. When they finally did, they elected Gregorio Papareschi, who took the name Innocent II. They couldn't use a traditional venue for the consecration because the Lateran and St. Peter's were both in the hands of the Pierleoni family, who

> ### ✂ ANTI-JEWISH POPE ✂
>
> **A number of cardinals took exception to Anacletus's Jewish roots, suspecting that he might still be practicing the Jewish faith in secret. This opposition also stemmed from the fact that certain parts of the Church were "in hock" to Roman Jewish moneylenders; the rebel cardinals saw the election of a quasi-Jewish pope as an attempt to undermine the authority of Roman Christianity.**

obviously supported Anacletus. So they were forced to move to the Church of Santa Maria Nuova, which was the titular church of Aimeric, the Roman chancellor. The service was conducted by the bishop of Ostia on February 23, 1130—the exact same day that Anacletus was consecrated.

✝ ✝ ✝

The *Annuario Pontificio* recognizes Anacletus as the legitimate pope and names Innocent as the antipope, but all subsequent Vatican texts declare the opposite.

✝ ✝ ✝

The result was an eight-year schism in the Church that was political as well as spiritual in nature. Anacletus was backed by the powerful Norman King Roger II of Sicily, whom he had actually crowned upon becoming pope. He had promised Roger lands in southern Italy, well beyond his Sicilian kingdom, in return for his support. Backed by such a formidable monarch, Anacletus looked unassailable, and Innocent fled to France. There, he began what today might be called a "charm offensive," winning the support of many of the medieval European monarchs. Among those who supported him were Louis VI of France and Henry I of England. He also received the partial support of the German monarch Lothair III, who dabbled on the side as the Holy Roman Emperor.

In return for his full support, Innocent promised Lothair the imperial crown and entitlement to certain papal lands in perpetuity. With Lothair's support, Innocent condemned Anacletus as a heretic and antipope at the Synod of Reims.

Innocent's position was made slightly easier in Rome by Anacletus's behavior. He had become even closer to Roger II of Sicily, creating fears of an invasion in southern Italy, and many deemed him overly friendly with Jewish moneylenders in the city. Since a number of churchmen were in debt to those same moneylenders, this did nothing to enhance his reputation. Rumors that the pope was secretly Jewish began to resurface once more; there were even reports that he'd been seen attending a synagogue on the outskirts of Rome. The popularity pendulum began to swing in Innocent's favor.

Lothair marched on Rome in the spring of 1133, but the supporters of Anacletus held out in part of the city, including St. Peter's. Consequently, Lothair had to be crowned in the Lateran Basilica on June 3. However, after the coronation he left Rome and returned to Germany, making Innocent's position in the city untenable. He fled to Pisa, where he issued excommunications against Roger and Anacletus. Christendom was now exposed to an appalling spectacle of threats and insults:

Anacletus was called "Jew pope" and "Jew lover," and his allegiance to the church was continually questioned.

The strife between the two men only ended in Anacletus's death in 1138. His choice for successor had been elected, taking the name Victor IV. Innocent was unremitting and threatened outright warfare, suggesting that Lothair might return and bombard the city—so Victor surrendered.

After his death, Anacletus was ultimately declared a "Jewish traitor to Christendom," and Innocent demanded that his name be stricken from the list of popes. However, like other controversial pontiffs, Anacletus still appears in some records as pope, in others as antipope, and in still others, not at all. Curiously enough, his younger brother would follow him as a legitimate pope, Lucius II (1144–1145).

WHEN NOBODY KNEW *WHO* WAS POPE

Alexander III (September 20, 1159–August 30, 1181)

In the history of the Church, there have been several occasions when multiple popes "reigned" simultaneously, such as during the Great Western Schism. The rivals typically denounced one another as antipopes, even though at least one must have been properly consecrated in the Lateran or St. Peter's. In this respect, the reign of Alexander III was a little different. For a while, nobody actually knew who was the pope, and although Alexander is now recognized as the legitimate pontiff, this wasn't always the case.

Born Orlando Bandinelli, Alexander had served as chancellor and as a papal legate under his predecessor Hadrian (Adrian) IV—the only Englishman ever to hold the papacy. A competent and industrious cardinal-priest, he had nevertheless made many enemies in that role. He was also a lawyer—the first ever to hold the office of pope—and this antagonized a number of people as well. At the time of his election, a handful of cardinals voted against him and instead supported Cardinal Ottaviano of Monticelli, but the greater number supported Bandinelli. Prior to the election, an agreement had been made that the pope could only be confirmed in his position if the vote had been

unanimous. As the vote was split for Bandinelli, he could not be confirmed as pontiff; but his supporters went ahead and confirmed him anyway, much to the alarm of his opponents, who were sympathetic toward the German Emperor Frederick Barbarossa. A violent dispute erupted. Cardinal Ottaviano's supporters suddenly broke into the room where Bandinelli was being confirmed and tore the red papal cloak from his shoulders, denouncing him as an antipope. The new pope had to seek refuge in the Vatican fortress beside St. Peter's, while his enemies prowled outside. A group of them then proceeded to the Lateran, where, backed by German forces, they proclaimed Cardinal Ottaviano the legitimate pope. He took the name Victor IV.

Alexander III was consecrated on September 20 in Ninfa, a village southeast of Velletri, by the bishop of Ostia; Victor IV was similarly enthroned at the imperial abbey at Farfa, northeast of Rome on October 4. Victor immediately announced that the new capital of the Church was Farfa, which significantly lay within German imperial territory. In support of Victor, the German Emperor convened a formal synod at Pavia in February 1160; fifty German bishops attending together with certain schismatic Italians. Unsurprisingly, they endorsed Victor IV,

excommunicated Alexander III, and denounced him as an anti-pope. Alexander, however, had already excommunicated Victor and now condemned the German Emperor.

With two seemingly legitimate popes each issuing edicts that the other denounced, no one knew who to follow. In October 1160, a synod in Toulouse assembled one hundred bishops and heads of monastic houses to resolve the situation. It was jointly chaired by Henry II of England and Louis VII of France, both of whom secretly supported Alexander. Both claimants to the papacy appeared before them and pressed their arguments for the papal throne. The convention found in support of Alexander and condemned Victor as an antipope. He then returned, in great anger, to Farfa and the bosom of the German Emperor Frederick Barbarossa.

Alexander returned to Rome, but the brooding presence of Frederick Barbarossa made it impossible to continue there. He left Italy for France in 1162 and set up court—along with his Curia—between 1163 and 1165. In the meantime, Victor also continued to reign as pope in Italy, treating Alexander as a usurper and demanding that Western Christendom abide by his edicts. Many, fearing the Germans, did so.

In 1165, however, Victor was seized with a sudden illness. This was an inconvenient turn of events for Frederick Barbarossa, as

it was soon time for his re-coronation and the coronation of his wife as empress, which only the pope could carry out. Frederick simply dismissed Victor and appointed a new pope, Paschal III, who would perform the ceremony. Paschal's consecration was carried out by two schismatic cardinals, two German bishops, and a prefect of Rome—and was considered legitimate. As Paschal was elected, Victor died. Hearing of his death, the Roman people invited Alexander to return to Rome, which he did in great triumph. His first act was to excommunicate Paschal, who in turn confirmed Alexander's own excommunication. Once again, nobody knew who was pope.

For three years, Alexander and Paschal continued to coexist as pontiffs, hurling insults and excommunications at one another, each declaring the other's edicts unlawful. Alexander held Rome, which seemed to give him some measure of authority. In 1168, Paschal suddenly died; but Frederick moved again and appointed another pope, Callistus III, who was once again confirmed by schismatic cardinals. He reigned as pope in Farfa until 1178. The shadow of the German Emperor still loomed large and Alexander was forced to flee to Benevento.

At the same time, Frederick Barbarossa's own position in Italy was actually weakening. A group of northern Italian

cities known as the Lombard League rose up against the German Emperor and defeated him at the Battle of Legnano in 1176. ✦ Lombard League: the union of Italian cities formed in 1167 to counteract the growing expansionism of the Holy Roman Emperor Frederick I into Italy. It comprised Milan, Piacenza, Cremona, Mantua, Crema, Bergamo, Brescia, Bologna, Padua, Trevi, Vicenza, Venice, Verona, and Lodi, and also included territories held by a number of Italian nobles, such as the Marquis Malaspina and Ezzelino da Romano. ✦ Hearing of their victory, Alexander rushed to give them his personal support; for this, the

✂ BITING THE HANDS THAT FED HIM ✂

As soon as he had achieved the full papacy, Alexander more or less turned on some of those who had supported him throughout his disputed pontificate. He is probably best remembered for imposing a penance on the English King Henry II—one of his staunchest supporters—in regard to the murder of St. Thomas Beckett. And in 1181, he placed the entire Scottish nation under interdict because King William the Lion had, in his view, meddled in Church appointments. This meant that no sacraments could be carried out in Scotland, a rule deemed exceptionally harsh since William, like Henry II, had supported him. The interdict was not lifted until the reign of Alexander's successor, Lucius III.

League named the new city of Alessandria in his honor. Frederick was now ready to talk terms. The emperor and the pope met in Venice, and Alexander agreed to lift the excommunication if Frederick would recognize him as pope and withdraw his support from Callistus. They reached an agreement, and in 1178, Pope Callistus made formal submission to Alexander, leaving him the undisputed pontiff.

In 1179, Alexander presided over the Third Lateran Council, which duly confirmed him as pope and put an end to any schism that existed in the Church. The papacy was back on track after quite a bit of confusion. However, that was but a prelude of what was to come in the Great Western Schism.

STRUCK OFF POPES

It is not unknown to have a pope's reign be struck off from Vatican records. This happened in a few cases, but most notably with Adrian V who was never even ordained as a priest, and John XXIII, who caused more problems than he solved.

Adrian V (July 11–August 8, 1276)

The pope who wasn't a priest

The brief reign and legitimacy of Adrian V presents something of a mystery. Was he qualified to be pope? Was he even a churchman? Certainly, Pope Paul VI did not seem to think so when in November 1976, he ordered Adrian's name to be struck from Vatican records on the grounds that he had never even been ordained as a priest. The *Annuario Pontificio*, however, still notes him as a legitimate pontiff. To add to the confusion, other sources show his papal reign as not lasting one month, but two years from 1274 to 1276, thus eliminating the reign of one of his predecessors, Innocent V, and cutting into part of the reign of Gregory X.

Born Ottobono Fieschi, Adrian was reputedly the nephew—more probably the illegitimate son—of Pope Innocent IV. At the time of his election, he was cardinal-deacon of the Church

of San Adriano, the name he would take as pope. However, it is not clear if he was ordained or had simply been "given" the position—either through bribes or through the offices of his uncle/father. Apparently, he had also served extremely successfully as a papal legate to England, returning to Rome to join the College of Cardinals and becoming one of its most outspoken and ambitious members.

After his election as pope, he assembled the cardinals and informed them that he was suspending the very strict rules for papal elections as laid down in the thirteenth century by Gregory X. This would open the papacy to non-clergy and to the possibility of even more bribery and corruption than was currently in operation. However, Adrian promised that new rules would be put in place to safeguard the dignity of the pontiff. He then set out from Rome to escape an oppressive summer. Up north in Viterbo, the pope suddenly became ill and died on August 18, 1276, amid rumors that he'd been poisoned. Although he hadn't been a particularly bad pope (his reign was not long enough to establish himself one way or the other), the question of his legitimacy persisted through the centuries until Paul VI finally settled the issue by ordering his name to be struck off. Whether or not it actually was remains another matter.

John XXIII (May 3, 1410–May 29, 1415)
The "embarrassment to the church" pope

When Pope John XXIII is mentioned today, most tend to think of the jolly and extremely popular Angelo Roncalli, cardinal of Santa Prisca and patriarch of Venice, who took the name in 1958. There was, however, *another* John XXIII, the name and number chosen by Cardinal Baldassare Cossa in the early fifteenth century. This particular John was excised from papal records as an "embarrassment to the Church," and it was prohibited to even speak of him again.

Perhaps the kindest thing that could be said about Cossa is that he did not have the temperament to be a pope. Born in Procida, one of the Phlegrean Islands off the coast of Naples, he had been a military man when he was younger. In this capacity, he had been both a soldier and a sailor—and at one point, even a pirate, raiding along the Sicilian coast. He loved food, wine, and, more importantly, beautiful women—tastes that would follow him into his pontificate. While in the military, he acquired a reputation as a philanderer and hedonist, and these allegations would taint his reign. He realized that there was more money to be made in the Church, so he gave up the military and prevailed upon some relatives to get him into the papal administration.

And he excelled despite a rather debauched lifestyle. In fact, he quickly rose through the ranks during Boniface IX's reign, becoming cardinal-deacon of St. Eustachius and later legate of Romandiola. He was also close to his successor, the weak and ineffective Gregory XII, making himself almost indispensable to the pope. However, the pope was not the ally that Cossa cultivated; he sought the patronage of the powerful French king, Louis of Anjou, who pledged to give him military support should he need it.

John's pontificate came at the end of what has become known as the Great Western Schism (see page 151), which had split the Church and produced a number of popes, each denouncing the other as a heretic and antipope. At this time, the pope in Rome was Gregory XII, an aging octogenarian. However, there was yet another pope in Avignon, France—Benedict XIII—who refused to recognize Gregory's election in December 1406. Gregory, in turn, called upon Benedict to abdicate and thus restore the unity of the Church; but the French pope had no intention of doing so. Worried about the damage that the Schism was doing to the Church, a number of cardinals suggested a meeting between the two pontiffs, and a conclave was set to be held by the following November in the city of Savona.

In the meantime, the ailing Gregory was urged not to relinquish the papacy, no matter what the outcome of these talks might be. This demand came from the kings of Naples, Bohemia, and Hungary as well as from his own nephews, who were greatly enjoying the benefits of having an uncle as pontiff. Benedict, too, had no intention of giving up the papacy, and he stalled regarding the proposed conclave. Under pressure from his nephews, Gregory made four of them cardinals in hopes that they would support him; but with the wealth they acquired, three abandoned him and fled to Pisa, where they joined several of Benedict's appointees and convened a conclave of their own. This turned into the 1409 Council of Pisa, which both Gregory and Benedict ignored, summoning councils of their own. However, the Council of Pisa had widespread support, and it condemned both popes for bad faith, corruption, and even collusion to destroy the unity of the Church for their own personal gain. At a third session held on June 5, the Council formally deposed both Gregory and Benedict and appointed a new pope, Alexander V. On hearing of the appointment, Gregory formally excommunicated Benedict and Alexander; but, in light of the hostility toward him, he was forced to flee from Rome disguised as a woman. He sought refuge with King Ladislas of Naples and was placed under the protection of the kings of Hungary and Bohemia.

To complicate matters even further, Alexander V died suddenly in May 1410, after less than a year on the papal throne and with the Council of Pisa still in session.

✝✝✝

Baldassare Cossa was one of the prime movers of the Council of Pisa, having followed Gregory's nephews in their ight from Rome and, despite Gregory's dependence upon him, was one of the first to turn against the aged pontiff. He skillfully manipulated the Council against his former patron, so that it would choose him as pope.

✝✝✝

The Council panicked and impulsively elected Baldassare Cossa, who took the name John XXIII.

As pontiff, John continued his debauches unchecked. Frequently drunk, he is alleged to have committed adultery, sodomy, and even incest. He is also accused of keeping his brother's wife in the Vatican as his mistress and of performing sexual congress on the papal throne. A number of cardinals spoke out against him, but they subsequently died—some under mysterious circumstances. The suspicion was that they were murdered on the orders of the pope. He threatened any dissenting monarch with his ally, Louis of Anjou. And once again, he verbally attacked the unfortunate Gregory, still in Naples, and forced King Ladislas

to expel the old man from the city. However, his relations with the Neapolitan monarch were extremely strained and, in 1413, Ladislas mounted an attack on the Roman coast, threatening Rome and forcing John and his cardinals to flee. He sought the protection of the German Emperor Sigismund—who was then trying to extend his power into Northern Italy—allegedly promising him papal lands in return for his support. This is a promise that John probably never intended to keep.

The death of Ladislas in 1414 allowed the pope to return to Rome, where he immediately resumed his debauched lifestyle. It is thought that he was also responsible for a minor crime wave that swept the city in the wake of the Neapolitan attack. However, his absence from Rome had given his enemies the chance to organize themselves against him.

As part of the bargain for Sigismund's protection, John had agreed to call the Council of Constance to end the Great Schism, which had seriously damaged the Church. But now that Ladislas was out of the way, John had no intention of implementing the Council. However, his enemies insisted that this was a formally constituted body convened by the German Emperor and that the pope must attend in person. John reluctantly set out for Constance, taking with him a

retinue of rather dubious followers that included prostitutes and known criminals.

The Council convened in November 1414 and would continue until April 1418. John's enemies used it to condemn the pope for his lax moral standards, his handling of the papacy, his alleged association with Roman crime, and his shameful treatment of the previous pope, Gregory XII. In the end, there could be only one outcome. In May 1415, the Council deposed John and elected Oddo Colonna, the cardinal-deacon of San Giorgio in Velabro, as pontiff. He took the name Martin V, and the Council immediately opened negotiations with the now-deposed Gregory XII, with a view to his abdication as pope. Gregory, over ninety years old at this point, was open to negotiations but died in the town of Recanati in October 1417.

Martin also considered the depraved behavior of his predecessor John XXIII; as punishment, the pope sent him to Tusculum as a cardinal-bishop responsible for the upkeep of several convents. It proved a foolish move, for Cossa allegedly seduced more than two hundred nuns (some of them quite elderly) and impregnated a number of them. It was Pope Nicholas V (1447–1455), the first of the Renaissance popes, who formally declared John XXIII an antipope. In an attempt

to finally consign the Western Schism to history, Nicholas decreed that because of his licentious behavior and disregard for his office, both John's name and pontificate should be completely excised from all Church records and never mentioned again. The only legitimate pope, he declared, had been Gregory XII. John XXIII was swiftly forgotten.

When Angelo Roncalli decided to adopt the name John in 1958, there was a constitutional panic; he was urged to reconsider and perhaps take another. However, Roncalli prevailed, becoming one of the most popular popes in history and removing the stigma that had attached itself to the title John XXIII.

SCHOLAR POPE

John XXI (September 8, 1276–May 20, 1277)

The only Portuguese pope to date, inaptly named Petrus Hispanus (Peter of Spain) was a renowned theological scholar. He is also the only medical man ever to hold the papacy. Born Pedro Julião around 1210, he took the name Peter of Spain to give himself some gravitas and status within the Church. It sounded, he said, like some of the ancient hermit fathers of the Church whom he wished to emulate. However, the name perhaps had more to do with his colossal academic vanity. He was cardinal-bishop of Tusculum when elected pope and was consecrated in the town of Viterbo less than ten days after the death of his predecessor Adrian V. Prior to becoming pope, he had taught medicine at the University of Siena and had been a personal physician to Gregory X (1272–1276). As a lecturer, he was used to deference from others and had an inflated sense of his own importance. He had also written an influential medical textbook on ophthalmology, *De Oculis (The Eye)*, as well as a widely read book on logic and a treatise on the soul. He was certainly accomplished and incredibly learned, but he was also aloof and condescending, considering himself intellectually superior to the cardinals who had elected him.

John's two predecessors, Innocent V and Adrian V, had only ruled just over six months between them, and difficulties were developing with the Eastern Church and the Byzantine Emperor. Political diplomacy and delicate administration were necessary under such circumstances. Because John considered himself a scholar, he refused to take any interest in the political and administrative aspects of his office, leaving the details of policy-making to Cardinal Giovanni Gaetano Orsini—a member of the influential Orsini family and the future Pope Nicholas III (1277–1280). Although Gaetano worked to reconcile the Latin and Greek churches, he was generally inept, and the indifference of the pope made his job much harder.

Throughout his reign, John shut himself away, immersed in study. He made a brief appearance to exhort the Christian monarchs and princes to mount another crusade that would liberate the holy places of Palestine from the occupying Saracens—a call that mostly went unheeded.

In the end, John's intellect was, in a sense, the death of him. He decided to have a small library built as an extension at the rear of the papal palace in Viterbo, to house his large collection of Scriptural works. In order to please the impatient pope, the library was constructed in haste. While John was studying there (some say he was sleeping), the ceiling caved in and the books piled against the walls fell, crushing him. He suffered serious injuries, from which he died two days later. It is therefore literally true to say that the pope was buried in his books.

WITCH POPE

Honorius III (July 24, 1216–March 18, 1227)

Although a number of popes have been accused of witchcraft, few have achieved the prominence of Honorius III. The taint of black magic on his reign persisted until as late as the seventeenth century.

Honorius could never match up to his predecessor, the great reforming Pope Innocent III (1198–1216); many of the kings who had pledged under Innocent to go on a Fifth Crusade (1217–1221) changed their minds under his successor. Consequently, the Crusade ended in total failure—as the previous one had—but this time Honorius was blamed. There were whispers that the pope had used sorcerer's powers to ensure that the campaign failed.

†††

As pope, Honorius was certainly interested in the occult, but this may have been from the aspect of preventing heresies rather than practicing witchcraft.

†††

Such suggestions played directly into the hands of his political enemies (the German Emperor Frederick II chief among them) and tainted the papacy with the idea of black magic.

After a series of disputes over whether or not Frederick would fight in the Crusade, the king began to spread rumors about Honorius—that he was incompetent and involved in sorcery. The pope, said the emperor, was an enemy of the Church seeking to undermine it through the dark arts. Although these stories remained only tittle-tattle, they made Honorius appear shifty and sinister. He may have been weak and indecisive but he was no black magician. The mud stuck and the pope found himself classed in many minds as a witch. However, he got his revenge: when Frederick eventually set sail on the Crusade in 1225, Honorius refused to make him head of the German forces. Instead he gave the papal authority to Oliver of Cologne, much to Frederick's fury.

In order to put an end to the rumors about him, Honorius formally backed Louis VIII of France in his campaign against the Albigensian heretics in the south of his country. Louis and Emperor Frederick, with the pope's approval, published ordinances that imposed severe penalties on heretics and laid the groundwork for the establishment of the Holy Inquisition. Even so, the taint of witchcraft clung to Honorius right up until his death in March 1227.

✂ WITCH AUTHOR? ✂

Even long after his death, Honorius's name continued to be associated with the occult and magic. In France during the 1600s, a *grimoire*, or book of evil magic, began to circulate under the title *The Grimoire of Pope Honorius III*. Attributed to the pope himself, the book is said to contain incantations used for the express purpose of raising demons and "fallen angels," all expressed in a quasi-Christian text. This, said some, was a distillation of the pope's knowledge, culled from ancient scrolls to which he alone was privy. The book is unquestionably a forgery, written long after Honorius was dead. However, the notion that Honorius was associated with it several centuries after his demise gives an indication as to how well Frederick's rumor mill had worked. The Pope may not have been a witch, but he certainly was an early victim of what today is called "spin," all of which was wholly unjustified.

BEWILDERED POPE

St. Celestine V (August 29–December 13, 1294)

Although poor, bewildered Celestine is often thought of as the only pope ever to resign from office, this is not correct. There were at least two popes who had done so before him, and indeed there may well have been more. However, the manner of both his election and his abdication made him something of a unique figure.

Born Pietro del Murrone in the Abruzzi region of Italy, he was the eleventh son of peasant parents. For most of his long life he was a simple Benedictine hermit and enjoyed a reputation for holiness. At the time of his election, he was already in his eighties.

In Rome, the papacy was in chaos following the death of Nicholas IV (1288–1292). For years, the office of the pope had fostered close ties with one of the major financial families in Rome, the Colonnas, but now that alliance was being challenged by another family, the Orsinis, who wanted to see a pope of their choice on St. Peter's throne. Amid all this, the Church was trying to assert *its* position, although there really was no suitable candidate. A small synod of cardinals, bribed by the Colonnas, met during a fiercely hot Italian summer in

1293, but they couldn't muster the required two-thirds to elect a pope. Then the Orsinis tried and fared no better. The deadlock needed a bold man to make a bold move—at last, one did.

Benedetto Caetani was cardinal-priest of San Martino and the possessor of a number of lucrative benefices, some of which he was alleged to have obtained by rather dubious means. He was also a very able papal lawyer. Seeing the confusion within the papacy, he decided to make a bid for the office himself, just as Charles II, King of Sicily and Naples, turned up the pressure in the hunt for a new pope. With no agreement in sight, the cardinals began to panic.

Caetani made his appearance in a rather dramatic way: he turned up at the conclave with a mysterious document written in an unidentified language. This, he claimed, was a letter from God that had been delivered by an angel, stating that the Divine Being wished *him* to be the next pope. The cardinals were understandably suspicious. They could not read the bizarre script and they did not trust Caetani, who claimed the letter could only be read by someone who was exceptionally holy; and this ruled out most of the Princes of the Church. The cardinals decided to take the letter to a person of unquestioned holiness, the hermit Peter of Morrone, who dwelt in a cave outside the city. So, at the

end of June 1294, a group journeyed into the hills to the cave of the hermit, bearing the letter. Peter examined it and declared that it was indeed from God; however, God's letter said that *he*, Peter, should be pope. The cardinals arrived back with this intelligence and proceeded to hold an election.

Benedetto Caetani was furious. He attempted to influence the vote through bribery and coercion, but gradually the cardinals swayed toward Peter. In order to speed things up, the hermit suddenly announced a vision in which God had told him that if the cardinals did not elect a new pope soon, they would all suffer divine retribution, as would the city of Rome itself. When the senior cardinal-dean announced that he was going to vote for Peter, the matter was settled. Peter of Morrone was nominated as pope, and he accepted the position, taking the name Celestine V.

The new pope entered Rome on August 28, riding a donkey in an imitation of Christ's entry into Jerusalem and to emphasize the humility of his papacy. He was immediately greeted by King Charles II of Sicily and Naples and escorted to the Church of Santa Maria di Collemaggio, where he was duly consecrated as pope. Immediately afterward, King Charles whisked him away, mediating all contact between him and the Roman Curia.

Charles also insisted that Celestine live not in Rome but in Naples, at the Castel Nuovo, where he could "be properly protected." Celestine raised no objection; indeed, the old man seemed to do whatever Charles told him to. He traveled to Rome rather infrequently and seemed to conduct most business from the Castel or from Charles's court, where he was an honored guest. He appointed several of Charles's men to key positions in the Church Curia and went so far as to name Charles's son, who was not a churchman, the archbishop of Lyons.

As an administrator, Celestine was hopeless. Unable to read or speak Latin—the language of the Vatican's machinery of state— and generally befuddled, he frequently named two people to the same benefices and signed the wrong documents. Alarmed at his ineptness and at the influence that the Sicilian king was exerting over him, the Curia insisted that he return to Rome. He briefly obeyed, a move that brought its own problems.

After years of living alone in a cave, the grandeur and pomp of the Vatican overwhelmed Celestine, who was still a simple monk at heart. He decided that it was far too magnificent a lifestyle to truly reflect the humility of Christ; therefore, to the horror of the Curia, he began to give away treasures and wealth of the Church to lowly beggars on Roman and Neapolitan streets.

It was a laudable and exemplary act of Christian charity, but one that seriously alarmed the Vatican financiers.

Celestine especially struggled when it came to the complicated Roman political landscape, with its feuding clans and underhanded duplicity. He promised one thing to one faction and then the same to another. It was not an act of deliberate duplicity, however, as the pope usually had no idea to whom he was speaking or the ramifications of what he was saying.

Taking advantage of the new pope's bewilderment and the growing frustration with him within the Curia, Benedetto Caetani, who was extremely skilled as a papal lawyer, suggested that he should resign. Of course, should this happen, Caetani planned to run for pope himself. Celestine replied that since God had instructed *him* to be pope, only God could instruct him to resign the office. Caetani tried another trick. Taking a room directly over the papal apartments, he drilled a small hole in the floor. Each night as Celestine retired, he would put his mouth to the hole and whisper "Celestine! Celestine! This is the voice of the Holy Spirit. The office that you have accepted is too great for you to bear! Give up the papacy and return to your hermitage! This is the express will of God! And you must also publicly name Benedetto Caetani as your successor. God wishes him to be the next pope."

For several nights, Caetani repeated these instructions until, at last, the bewildered pope decided that he should abdicate. Celestine accepted the formula for resignation that Caetani had prepared for him, and the pope abandoned the throne, leaving the way open for the unscrupulous lawyer. However, those who supported Celestine and who suspected what Caetani was doing questioned the validity of the resignation and urged him to stay. Celestine was adamant, believing that God had instructed him to give up the papacy. He allowed himself to be stripped of his robes and his papal insignia and advised the cardinals to make haste to find his successor. His departure provoked a conflict

between rival factions that resulted in the election of Benedetto Caetani as Pope Boniface VIII.

When the lawyer became pope, he made sure that Celestine did not return to his hermitage as he had wished. Fearful that the old man would become a rallying point for the new pope's enemies and provoke a schism, he had Celestine arrested and placed under guard after being thrown into a cell in Castel Fumone, east of Ferentino. The old man managed to escape for two months but ultimately died there from an abscess that had turned septic.

Celestine was buried in Ferentino, but his remains were transferred in 1517 to Santa Maria di Collemaggio in L'Aquila, where he had been crowned as pope. He was later canonized by Pope Clement V, under direct orders of the French King Philip IV, who had been a dedicated opponent of Boniface VIII.

EGOTISTICAL POPE

Boniface VIII (January 20, 1295–October 11, 1303)

Benedetto Caetani, or Boniface VIII, was known by his contemporaries as a scheming, vicious, and thoroughly nasty pope. He had tricked his predecessor Celestine V into renouncing the papacy and was elected through a mixture of bribes, promises, and threats. He chose the name Boniface and the number VIII even though the previous incumbent of that name—Boniface VII (974 and 984–985)—had been an antipope.

✝✝✝

The pope may have called himself Boniface, but he certainly did not have a "bonny face." Pinched and perpetually scowling, the new pope hardly presented an approachable figure.

✝✝✝

As soon as he became pope, Boniface dismissed all the appointments of his predecessor, and those who disagreed were subject to the full force of his irascible temper. He had grandiose ideas about himself and his holy office, dressing in full pontifical robes no matter how small the occasion and declaring himself as powerful as any monarch or emperor. Moreover, he treated everyone who came near him with a disdainful attitude,

which enraged many of the powerful Roman families. On top of this, he authorized the erection of so many statues of himself around Rome that he was accused of fostering idolatry in the Roman people.

Above all, Boniface had wildly inflated ideas about his role on the world's political stage. He tried to intervene in affairs in Sicily, where rebels had ousted the legitimate King Charles II of Naples, and transferred the monarchy to the House of Aragon. In this, he failed spectacularly, as he did in his efforts to mediate a dispute between the city-states of Venice and Naples. He then faithfully promised Charles that he would secure the Hungarian crown for his grandson; but again, his efforts came to naught. Almost glibly he promised to secure the independence of Scotland from England; his failure drew antagonism from the English court.

The main confrontation in Boniface's pontificate, however, was with Philip IV (Philip the Fair) of France, a man who was as self-important as the pope himself. Boniface had no love for the French king and first tried to undermine him by forbidding taxation of the clergy, upon which Philip relied to finance his foreign wars. An imperious papal bull, *ClericisLaicos*, was issued on February 25, 1296, and was unquestionably

aimed at the French ruler. Philip retaliated by forbidding the export of gold from French ports, on which the papacy depended, forcing the pope into a humiliating climb-down in order to reinstate the tax. Philip was now free to levy taxation from the clergy without having to consult the Holy See. Boniface then tried to intervene in the war between France and England—seemingly anxious to mediate but actually slyly trying to negotiate terms favorable to the English. The move failed, as the English had as little love for the pope as the French, and all Boniface did was further antagonize the French court. He was once more forced into a humiliating position, having to canonize Philip's grandfather, Louis IX, very much against his own wishes.

In Rome, Boniface's haughtiness angered the influential Colonna family, who had initially supported his election. In order to destabilize his reign, they circulated the idea that Celestine V had not abdicated according to proper procedure and might still actually be pope. In great anger, Boniface demanded that the castles of two Colonna cardinals be seized. They refused and declared the papacy for Celestine, proclaiming that Boniface's election had been illegal. Boniface then excommunicated both cardinals on the grounds that they had questioned papal authority, and he allegedly hired mercenaries to murder them. The two

fled Italy and took refuge at the court of Philip IV, fuelling antipathy toward the papacy.

Nevertheless, Boniface ignored all this and became even more grandiose in his ways, eventually declaring himself more important than any temporal ruler. In 1301, he reignited his feud with Philip IV, who immediately imprisoned the bishop of Palmiers, reducing him to the status of a layperson without any reference to the pope. Considering this an affront to his spiritual authority, Boniface convened a synod to denounce and excommunicate the French king. Thirty-nine French bishops obeyed the pope's call despite Philip's order not to. From this synod emerged the papal bull *Unam Sanctum*, by which Boniface reasserted his authority and concentrated yet more power in his own hands. The synod stopped short of excommunicating Philip, although it did censure him.

Philip responded with a tirade of abuse directed against the pope. His charges, all of which were probably true, included simony, sexual misconduct, blasphemy, usurping the papal office, and heresy. Not content with lambasting the pontiff, Philip also called for a grand council to impeach and depose him.

Despite his haughtiness and inflated self-image, Boniface had no wish to face such a gathering, nor had he any wish to let

outsiders look too closely into his affairs. After preparing a bull of excommunication against the king, he fled Rome for the papal palace at Agani, the city of his birth. He was pursued by armed mercenaries in Philip's pay; they stormed the palace and took Boniface prisoner.

✝ ✝ ✝

Even in captivity, Boniface remained aloof, still dressing in full pontifical robes, and treated his captors with a cold disdain—he *was* the pope, after all!

✝ ✝ ✝

The plan was to take him directly to France, where he would have been under Philip's personal control and where he could be tried as a common criminal. But the citizens of Agani managed to rescue him after three days. Boniface demanded that he be returned to the papal palace right away and dismissed his

---

⚷ KISS OF DEATH ⚷

Boniface is believed by some historians to have invented the pope's ring—a device with a poisoned spike on its lower side that pricked the skin of enemies as they knelt to kiss it in a symbol of subservience to the pontiff—although its invention has been attributed to a number of other popes as well.

rescuers without any reward or recognition. They could be content, he told them, that they had done God's work by rescuing his foremost servant. Boniface returned to Rome after a period of rest; but with his spirit crushed, he died less than three weeks later on October 12, 1303. He was buried in the crypt of St. Peter's Basilica. Allegedly, his tomb was opened in 1605 and his body was found intact and uncorrupted, a discovery that might have qualified him for sainthood if anyone had been interested in pursuing the cause.

PLAYBOY POPES

From putting on elaborate festivals and carnivals to drinking too much to sex, sex, and more sex, some popes just didn't know when to stop. While many popes were guilty of overdoing it, Clement VI and Paul II were especially grievous in their playboy ways.

Clement VI (May 7, 1342–December 6, 1352)
The pope who was "drunk as a pope"

Very few Vicars of Christ can outdo the French Pope Clement VI when it comes to hedonism, drinking, and living the good life. Clement's reign inspired the expression "drunk as a pope," which certainly reflected the easy-going worldly style of this playboy pontiff.

Clement was the fourth Avignon pontiff during the "Babylonian captivity" of the papacy. ✦ Babylonian captivity: a period during which the Israelites were held in Babylon under the reign of Nebuchadnezzar II (586 BC). The term was mostly used by the Roman Church to refer to the Avignon Papacy during the Western Schism. ✦ Born Pierre Roger, he served as the Benedictine archbishop of Rouen, the chancellor of France, and the cardinal-priest of the church of Santi Nereo e Achilleo at the time of his election as pope. To ensure that he was elected, French King

Philip VI sent his son to the conclave of cardinals, but his presence and influence were not needed. Stifled by the rigid authoritarianism of Clement's predecessor, Benedict XII, the cardinals wanted a change in both direction and tone. They certainly got that. In a unanimous election, Clement declared that he wished to make the papacy "more accessible"—and that he did.

Shortly after he became pope, Clement received a request to return the papacy to Rome; he refused, wishing to stay where he was and where he had access to a variety of hedonistic pleasures. In fact, he actually purchased the city of Avignon on behalf of the papacy from Queen Joanna I of Naples and set about enlarging the papal palace there. He appointed only Frenchmen to the College of Cardinals, ensuring that they would do his bidding. As a monk, Clement had allegedly been rather renowned for his piety, but he would abandon this as soon as he reached Peter's chair; one would be hard-pressed to say his pontificate resembled the life of the apostle in any way. He loved luxury, and his reign was punctuated by sumptuous banquets and spectacular festivals. His frugal predecessor Benedict had built up the Vatican coffers, and Clement now shamelessly depleted them.

Politically, he was fortunate. Shortly after he came to the papal throne, the German Emperor Louis IV, one of his great

enemies, suddenly died in 1347. Taking advantage of the situation and of Louis's unpopularity, Clement backed Charles, the king of Bohemia and Luxembourg, to succeed him, even though Louis's sons backed Otto of Schwartzburg, another of Clement's critics. With the pope's backing, Charles succeeded to the German throne and provided an ally for the hedonistic pope. With the formidable Charles on his side, few others dared criticize the pontiff too publicly.

The pope kept a harem of French whores about his chambers, and there were also persistent rumors that he greatly enjoyed the company of young boys and was caught several times with married women.

✝ ✝ ✝

Rumor has it that the pope was treated on numerous occasions for syphilis, insisting each time that the physicians be blindfolded so they wouldn't recognize him.

✝ ✝ ✝

A consummate wine lover, he was frequently unable to say Mass due to his advanced state of intoxication.

As the black death swept into Avignon in 1348 and 1349, Clement withdrew to the countryside to escape the worst effects of the plague. He died in December 1352 after a short illness,

but not before he had defended the Jews of the city who were accused of poisoning Christian wells—the last charitable act of an otherwise self-indulgent and licentious playboy pope. He was buried in the Cathedral of Avignon, but his remains were later transferred to the Benedictine abbey of La Chaise-Dieu, where he had wished to be buried. His grave was desecrated by the Huguenots in 1562, and his bones were burned as an act of defiance against the papacy.

Paul II (August 30, 1464–July 26, 1471)
Torture, racketeering, and sex, oh my!

Although "playboy pope" could be used to describe any number of pleasure-seeking pontiffs, Paul II was surely one of the most committed to having fun. Prior to his election, there had been a number of rather "worldly" pontiffs and the Curia was now looking for someone who would be more committed to Church reform. Consequently, they spelled out what they wanted in an eighteen-point electoral pact, defining a scheme of work for the next pope and calling for the establishment of various councils to consider reform, including a resumption of the war against the Turks. When Cardinal Barbo, the cardinal-priest of San Marco, was unexpectedly elected (probably through bribery), he stated that

the pact was only a guideline and therefore he was not bound to follow it. Barbo also toyed with taking the name Formosus II—a tribute to the dead pope who had been put on trial by the infamous Cadaver Synod in January 897 (see "The Exhumed Pope," page 55)—but the public outcry persuaded him otherwise.

Paul II was arguably the worst of the Renaissance pontiffs—vain, intellectually shallow, and extremely ostentatious in his lifestyle. There were frequent rumors that he was bisexual and that he derived gratification from watching male prisoners being tortured. This led to allegations that he performed "wicked acts in public view," probably masturbation, at the torture-filled interrogations of heretics, which the pope continually attended.

A promoter of carnivals, he forced the Roman Jews to contribute to their expense under pain of attack and threats of closure to their businesses. He ran what might best be described today as extortion and racketeering enterprises all across Rome and consorted closely with the city's criminals.

†††

The pope lost the respect of the city's intellectuals by abolishing a College of Papal Draftsmen, which, despite its title, was filled with literary figures.

†††

As his pontificate wore on, he became more and more disliked by the Roman people.

Like some of his predecessors, Paul did try to mount a crusade against the expanding Turkish Empire and called on the Christian kings of Europe to support him financially. His efforts bore little fruit, however, partly because he pocketed most of the money that was raised. The King of Bohemia eventually suspected what was going on and threatened to expose him, whereupon Paul excommunicated the monarch on the grounds that he was an alleged Hussite (Protestant). The pope's call for a crusade against the king's people was not carried out. Instead, the kings of Germany and France called for the establishment of the Council of Constance to investigate the matter. Fearing it would expose his own shady dealings, the pope delayed the council until the monarchs forgot about it. Others who opposed Paul or spoke out against his playboy ways were arrested and tortured. He was especially antagonistic toward the Vatican librarian Bartolomeo Platina, demanding he write a glowing account of his life that portrayed him as a saint. He even went so far as to imprison and torture Platina in order to ensure his compliance. Paul II died suddenly of a stroke at the age of fifty-four in July 1471. On his death, Platina exacted his revenge by writing a highly unfavorable biography of the late pope. The playboy pontiff was buried with worthier men in St. Peter's.

UNSTABLE POPE

Urban VI (April 8, 1378–October 15, 1389)

While madness was not an uncommon trait of popes through-out history, the pontificate of Urban VI displayed a rather subtle mental instability. He was born Bartolomeo Prignano and was archbishop of Bari before being elected pope by a factious and rowdy conclave in 1378.

✝ ✝ ✝

Urban was the last non-cardinal to become pope.

✝ ✝ ✝

Before being elected, Prignano had been considered a con-scientious and able administrator—but he also had a dark and unstable side. Subject to violent mood swings and an almost maniacal temper, by the summer of 1376, Urban had alienated almost all of the cardinals who had elected him. Declaring that the College should *only* consist of Italians and that all other nationalities should be barred from the papacy forever, he threatened to kick all French cardinals out. It was, of course, a dangerous political stance, but those who pointed this out were met with a tirade of filthy and obscene abuse from the pope.

✝ ✝ ✝

When the pope was *really* mad he would physically attack those who disagreed with him, beating and kicking them while simultaneously berating them with appalling language.

✝ ✝ ✝

Alarmed and angered by the pontiff's behavior, the French cardinals withdrew to consider their options.

On August 1, at the prompting of the French contingent, the College of Cardinals published a declaration claiming that Urban's election had been invalid, and they invited the pope to abdicate. Urban, of course, refused and greeted the invitation with a string of obscenities. Five days later, the College sent out a letter to all of Christendom, stating that the pope had been deposed and that the person sitting in Peter's chair was an intruder who should not be heeded. Again, Urban responded with obscenities. It was a mortal sin to disobey him, he said, punishable by excommunication—indeed, he threatened to excommunicate the entire Curia if they did not acknowledge him as pontiff.

In response, the French cardinals elected Robert of Geneva, the French king's cousin, who took the name Clement VII. And thus began the Great Western Schism (see page 151). With

Europe badly divided between the two popes, Urban began to muster the military might of those who had remained loyal to him, and they forged a papal army. Clement did the same. The two forces met in bloody conflict near Marino in April 1379, with Urban's troops winning the battle and capturing Castel Sant'Angelo, securing control of Rome itself. Clement retreated south toward Naples and from there, fled to Avignon where he set up a magnificent court and continued to reign as pope. The two men did not meet again, although they exchanged insults and excommunicated one another.

The conclusion of Urban's pontificate was just as unstable as the rest of it. He became fixated on removing his enemies from office. He also became greatly preoccupied with obtaining the kingdom of Naples for a relative. The fact that the kingdom already had a ruling monarch—Queen Joanna—did not overly burden him. In 1380, he excommunicated Joanna on the grounds that she had expressed some sympathy for the antipope Clement, and he replaced her with his cousin Charles of Durazzo, whom he personally crowned as monarch. However, Charles was rather hostile toward Urban, believing him to be, at best, unstable or, at worst, mad. He then began to plot with a number of cardinals to remove him from office. On hearing of this, Urban immediately

excommunicated Charles, stripping him of his titles, and placed an interdict on Naples. ✦ Interdict: the removal of spiritual and sacramental benefits. ✦ He ordered a crusade against Charles and personally led a force against him. But Charles was a much more skilled commander than the pope, and he besieged Urban at Nocera. Urban managed to escape and fled to Genoa with six loyal cardinals. Once there, he turned against *them* for no apparent reason, and had them thrown into jail and brutally tortured. Five of them were executed on Urban's orders.

Charles died in Hungary in 1386, and in 1387, Urban moved to Pisa, where he attempted to recruit mercenary soldiers for a campaign against Naples, which now openly supported his papal rival Clement. However, the Vatican coffers were empty and the pope couldn't raise sufficient funds to muster a credible army; the campaign foundered. In October 1388, he left Pisa and returned to Rome, where his continued erratic behavior soon engendered the hatred of both the Church and the Roman people.

The Vatican was in chaos and the Papal States were threatening revolt. Urban paid these matters no heed but continued to plot against Naples and against Clement in Avignon. On October 15, 1389, he suddenly died, probably from poisoning.

Urban left the Church badly split, the papal lands in a state of upheaval, and Christendom at a particularly low point. At the time of his death, Clement VII was still alive, but no attempt was made to offer him St. Peter's chair or to recognize him as a legitimate pope. The Great Schism that Urban created was set to rumble on for almost another fifty years.

THE GREAT WESTERN SCHISM (1378–1415)

The Great Schism of the fourteenth and early fifteenth centuries was the most serious split to affect the Church in the West for many years. Its origins, however, were political rather than theological.

Traditionally, the pope is inextricably linked with Rome—indeed, he is the *Bishop of Rome*—and today, he administrates from that city. This has not always been the case. From June 1305 until March 1375, the papal court resided in the city of Avignon, France, thanks to a series of French popes who had relocated the throne to their own country. The period is usually referred to as "the Babylonian captivity" of the Church, and it would lay the ground for what would become known as the Great Western Schism of 1378–1415.

The rot set in almost seventy years earlier with the pontificate of Benedict XI, who is described as "scholarly but weak" and who had more or less become the pawn of the powerful French king, Philip IV (Philip the Fair). Philip had frequent political clashes with Benedict's predecessor, Boniface VIII, and he wasn't about to repeat the confrontation with his successor.

† † †

Boniface VIII was a powerful and imperialist pontiff who had tried to seriously limit the French monarch's powers.

† † †

So he ensured that Benedict would do what he was told and that the Vatican would become an extension of the French Court.

When Benedict died after a brief two-year reign, Philip engineered a French successor, Bertrand de Got, who took the name Clement V. Clement suffered from cancer and was forced to withdraw from public life for long periods. In 1309, he retired to Avignon, partly for his own health and partly at the insistence of Philip, who advised him to conduct papal affairs from there. The French king wanted the papacy close to the French court, where it could be more easily manipulated and where he could take political advantage of Clement's frequent bouts of ill health. Clement would be the first French pontiff to rule from France— kicking off the era of "Babylonian captivity" that lasted until the reign of Gregory XI (1371–1378), who moved the papacy back to Rome at the prompting of St. Catherine of Sienna. The return to Italy, of course, did not sit terribly well with the highly corrupt Avignon popes who had built up a lavish court in France and whose interests lay there.

Gregory's successor, Urban VI (see page 146), was so unstable and volatile that his reign gave the French cardinals an opportunity to consider reestablishing the papacy in France. In 1378, they invited Urban to abdicate, planning to elect a successor in Avignon; when he refused, they went ahead anyway. In the town of Fondi, they elected Robert of Geneva, the French king's cousin, as pope on September 20. He took the name Clement VII and on October 31, he moved to excommunicate Urban and declare himself the rightful pope. Urban, in turn, excommunicated Clement and declared him an antipope. These actions effectively split the Church.

Urban's irascible and unstable nature only served to exacerbate the conflict. He ranted and berated his Curia until many of themdefected and joined a rival grouping under Clement. In the meantime, the French pope was setting up his own court, using the defecting members of the Curia and naming twenty-nine

✂ EUROPEAN LOYALTIES WERE DIVIDED ✂

Clement	Neutral	Urban
France, Burgundy, Naples, Savoy, and Scotland.	Initially, Spain remained neutral, although Catherine of Sienna supported Urban.	Most of Italy, Scandinavia, Germany, Portugal, England, Hungary, Poland, and much of Central Europe.

new cardinals of varying nationalities. When excommunications and denunciations of heresy didn't work, the two pontiffs began amassing and arming mercenary forces—which, sure enough, resulted in outright battles. The most significant took place in Marino, Italy, in April 1379. Urban's forces won. Amid growing fears that the Church would be irrevocably ripped asunder, several attempts were made to broker peace deals; but Urban, wholly convinced of his own papal legitimacy, refused to compromise. Urban died in 1389 with Clement still incumbent in France.

Urban's successor Boniface IX (1389–1404) did relatively nothing to resolve the Schism, although he did offer to make Clement a legate to France if he would renounce his pontificate. When Clement refused, Boniface began strengthening ties with England and Germany, in many ways deepening the split. He appealed once again to the French pope to stand down, but Clement died in 1394 without ever agreeing to his terms.

The new Avignon pope, Benedict XIII, was thoroughly convinced of the legitimacy of his claim to the papacy; but he nevertheless tried to open channels of communication with Boniface, who ignored every attempt. Even the French king withdrew recognition from the Avignon papacy for five years, in reaction to Benedict's refusal to honor the Avignon cardinals' oath to stand

down if the majority judged it proper to do so. On the other hand, Boniface's blatant nepotism and outright financial skulduggery turned many against *him* and ensured that Benedict still retained plenty of support. In September 1404, a delegation from Benedict arrived in Rome with a startling proposal—that *both* popes would abdicate for the good of the Church and let a successor be chosen. However, Boniface was too ill to receive the delegates. A second meeting on September 29 was inconclusive and marked by violent exchanges. Boniface died two days later.

As the new pope, Innocent VII (1404–1406), took office, the antipope Benedict arrived in Rome, suggesting face-to-face meetings in an attempt to end the Schism. Innocent refused and was unwilling to cooperate with his rival, a move he felt would give undue credence to Benedict.

✝ ✝ ✝

Benedict had asked Innocent to postpone his election in order to engage in a dialogue first, but Innocent believed that even meeting with Benedict would legitimize the antipope's position, something he did not want to do.

✝ ✝ ✝

Toward the end of the year, however, he reluctantly summoned a synod to consider the problem—a gesture to appease the newly

elected king of Germany—but it never took place due to rioting in Rome. The Schism rumbled on without resolution for the rest of Innocent's two-year reign.

With the 1406 election of his successor, Gregory XII, the Great Western Schism widened even more: there were now *three* popes vying for office. The Church had grown weary of the situation, so the Council of Constance convened to depose the antipope John XXIII (see "Struck Off Popes: John XXIII," page 114). But the Council had more business to attend to. It opened negotiations with Gregory and convinced him to abdicate his office. Then it declared the Avignon Pope Benedict XIII a heretic and deprived him of all papal rights when he refused to do the same. They went on to elect the next pope, Oddo Colonna, cardinal-deacon of San Giorgio in Velabro, who took the name Martin V. Benedict XIII continued to "rule" from Avignon, although his edicts were invalid and nobody paid him any attention. His successor, Clement VIII, continued to hold out while his following dwindled; in 1429, he was forced to renounce his claim to the papacy and submit to Martin. The thirty-nine-year Schism was finally over for good. However, it had been extremely damaging for the future of Catholic Christianity in the West and certainly added fuel to the fire for the emerging Protestant movement.

DEBAUCHED POPES

Many popes did not lead the holiest lives, but two consecutive popes take the cake for having the most debauched reigns: Innocent VII and Alexander VI. They frequented in bribery, simony, and nepotism and made virtual whorehouses out of the Vatican that resulted in several illegitimate children. They also did their fair share of torture and killing, truly pulling the Church down to the lowest depths of debauchery.

Innocent VIII (August 29, 1484–July 29, 1492)
Not so innocent after all

With the pontificate of Innocent VIII, the papacy plumbed new depths of debauchery, laying the foundation for the even more hedonistic papal reign that followed. There was nothing holy about Innocent's time in office, nor anything to distinguish the Vatican from the court of a sensual, worldly prince.

Born Giovanni Battista Cibo, the former cardinal-priest of Santa Cecilia and bishop of Molfetta was only elected to the papacy because the nephew of the previous pope, Cardinal Giuliano della Rovere, wanted someone in the position whom he could dominate.

Innocent VIII was the father of at least three illegitimate children prior to his consecration as pontiff.

The conclave that elected Innocent was riddled with intrigue, bribery, and blackmail. Because of the immense debts left by his predecessor Sixtus IV, the Vatican coffers were low. But Innocent wished to maintain a lavish lifestyle, so he had to use unscrupulous methods to raise money. He was enthusiastically aided by the cardinals who themselves wished to live in a grand and extravagant style. Innocent held auctions for existing offices within the Curia and created new and unnecessary offices to sell off at exorbitant prices. This was, of course, the sin of simony, against which several previous popes had spoken out, but Innocent granted himself absolution and continued to sin. He increased papal taxation without any explanation or need and established new "donations" to the Church, which many Roman businesses were forced to pay.

Perhaps persuaded by Giuliano della Rovere, Innocent rather foolishly challenged the power of Neapolitan King Ferdinand I, who had refused to pay the recently raised papal taxes. Allying himself with some barons who were opposed to the king,

Innocent threatened Ferdinand and tried to provoke war. The alliance of barons collapsed, the rebellion crumbled, and the pope was forced to make a humiliating and personally distasteful peace with Ferdinand in 1486.

✝ ✝ ✝

Like a number of other popes, Innocent had several mistresses; some of them bore his children, whom he openly acknowledged.

✝ ✝ ✝

Having made peace with Ferdinand, the pope now tried to undermine the monarch's reign by leaguing with the powerful Roman house of Medici. His son Franceschetto was married to the daughter of Lorenzo de' Medici, and to secure Medici aid, the pope made their thirteen-year-old son—his grandson—a cardinal. In 1489, Ferdinand broke the peace, giving Innocent the chance he wanted. With Medici aid, he deposed Ferdinand and excommunicated him. However, the Neapolitans were able to retain the important principality of L'Aquila, now lost to the papacy and one of Innocent's more enduring failures.

In order to divert attention from the hedonism and incompetence of his reign, Innocent sought out a scapegoat for the evils that were besetting Rome and parts of Europe. Trying to appear as a deeply religious, reforming pope, he launched a crusade against

sorcery and witchcraft, which he claimed were everywhere. His main targets were witches in Germany who, he claimed, were poisoning all of Europe. Innocent strengthened the arm of the Holy Inquisition and commissioned Heinrich Kramer (former senior Inquisitor in the Tyrol) and theologian Jacob Sprenger to write the Church's foremost manual against witchcraft, *Malleus Maleficarum* (*The Hammer of the Witch*), which has remained a classic ever since. Innocent's crusade brought about mass burnings and killings in Germany and elsewhere—many elderly women and some children as young as four years old were victims.

In another attempt to divert attention from his corrupt and carnal ways, Innocent began to preach a crusade against the Turks, as many popes before him had done. However, his greed got the better of him: in exchange for bribes and gifts, he made peace with the Turkish sultan in contravention of his own call. He also accepted the sultan's half-brother (a rival for the sultanate) as a hostage together with a personal payment of forty thousand ducats per year. ✦ Ducat: a gold trade coin used all across Europe until World War I. Its value varied depending on where it was minted. ✦ In addition, Innocent received the legendary Spear of Longinus—which had allegedly pierced the side of Christ while on the cross—along with several other

treasures. A bit of respite was offered with the news that the Moorish caliphate of Granada had fallen to Christian forces in Spain. In a show of religious fervor, Innocent promptly proclaimed the Spanish King Ferdinand, Queen Isabella, and their descendants as "Catholic monarchs" before returning to his drinking and whoring.

But his hedonistic lifestyle was taking its toll—the pope, now frequently drunk, was becoming weaker and less able to fulfill his duties. Three days before Christopher Columbus reached the coast of America, Innocent fell ill. As he lay dying on July 25, 1492, he told the cardinals around his bed that his reign had been one of debauchery and sin and begged them to elect a better pope. It's a pity that they didn't heed him.

Alexander VI (August 26, 1492–August 18, 1503)
It started with a bad name

If Innocent was bad, his successor was destined to become one of the most notorious popes in history.

✝ ✝ ✝

Alexander VI's original surname, Borgia, has become a byword for nepotism, greed, and carnal desire.

✝ ✝ ✝

The second of two Spanish popes, he was born Rodrigo de Borja y Borja (or Borgia, in its Italian translation) and was a nephew of Pope Callistus III, who had made him a cardinal-deacon at the age of twenty-five. In this position, he was able to accumulate great wealth and was counted to be the second-richest cardinal in Rome at the time of his elevation to the papacy. He made no secret of his wealth and influence and, during his time as cardinal-deacon, lived an openly promiscuous life that ill-befitted a Prince of the Church. By the time he was made pope, he had openly fathered a number of illegitimate children, and he continued to do so while in Holy Office.

Rodrigo was a creature of the court of Innocent VIII—greedy, ambitious, wholly corrupt, a skilled manipulator, and a man with an eye for intrigue and opportunity. He had hoped to succeed Innocent's predecessor, Sixtus IV, but had to wait until the conclave of 1492 to secure the votes he needed. This he did with a mixture of bribes, threats, and intimidation, together with promises of lucrative benefices and placements to certain key churchmen. His election was therefore simoniacal (purchased) and technically a sin. It could have quite properly been declared invalid, but nobody thought to challenge the new pope.

Taking the name Alexander VI, he was crowned in St. Peter's in August 1492. His choice of papal name is an interesting one. Technically, he should have called himself Alexander V, since the original Alexander V had been declared an antipope.

Alexander VI made a promising start, inevitably calling for a crusade against the Turks, restoring order to a troubled Roman city, and promising to reform the corrupt Curia. Nevertheless, it soon became evident that the pope was more concerned with impregnating female consorts, acquiring wealth for himself and his family, and doling out positions and privileges to his relatives than with sacred matters. The pattern of nepotism had been well and truly bedded down in the papacy during the reign of Sixtus VI (1472–1484), who shamelessly handed out positions to many family members and illegitimate children of his mistresses. But Alexander took the idea to new levels. For example, he made one son, Cesare, a cardinal at the age of eighteen, even though he was linked to gambling rackets and extortion throughout Rome. He further doled out favors to his mistresses' relatives, making the brother of a whore a cardinal and handing out Church benefices to the family of several others.

†††

In his brief ten-month reign, Alexander V had been associated with the discredited Baldassare Cossa, the antipope John XXIII—see page 114—during the Great Western Schism. His devious politicking had angered Gregory XII (1406–1415), who denounced and excommunicated him, ordering his name to be posthumously struck from Vatican records. However, Alexander's status as an antipope was still a vexed question and Rodrigo Borgia obviously did not pay any heed to the controversy.

†††

In a hypocritical show of religious fervor, the pope declared he would make the Curia "more accountable" and "more in the image of Christ." But the move had nothing at all to do with holiness. It was a cynical ploy to limit the power of wealthy Roman families who had dominated the papacy in the past and to establish a papal dynasty for his own family. In fact, he had already planned for his son Juan to succeed him as pope.

While visiting concubines away from Rome, Alexander often left the papacy in the hands of his daughter Lucrezia. During these periods, she acted as virtual ruler of the city and had full papal powers, conferred upon her by her father. He arranged several advantageous marriages for her to wealthy and influential husbands, all of whom died shortly afterward in mysterious circumstances.

Perhaps Alexander's best-known political act is linked to the New World. In 1493, he was called to adjudicate on the matter of the territories, which were to be explored by Spain and Portugal. It was he who drew the line of demarcation between the designated areas. This decision had to be revised the following year, as the pope had unsurprisingly erred in favor of the Spanish.

Alexander proclaimed himself a patron of the arts—not unusual for Renaissance popes, as human art was one way in which the glory of God could be made manifest. In Alexander's case, however, this was a cynical maneuver, as most of the work carried out "for the glory of God" was on the Borgia apartments in the Vatican. His own rooms were sumptuously decorated by the celebrated Umbrian painter Pinturicchio, and he even persuaded Michelangelo to draw up plans for the rebuilding of St. Peter's to his own liking.

Meanwhile, Alexander's personal life became more and more scandalous: prostitutes came and went from the Vatican with

an almost monotonous regularity and, like John XII before him, he is rumored to have carried out sexual congress on the papal throne itself. When the famous Florentine preacher and reformer Girolamo Savonarola called for Alexander's overthrow and a return to moral ways, the pope's response was excommunication, then arrest, torture, and finally execution. This, he said, would prevent anyone else from criticizing the pope. But the horrific punishment of Savonarola in 1498 caused many to turn against Alexander. Even so, with many now afraid of him, the pope continued to squander Vatican money on a lavish lifestyle and increasing hordes of prostitutes.

Following the 1497 death of his favorite son and planned successor Juan, Alexander was so devastated that he publicly vowed to lead a more upright life and concern himself with Church reform.

✝✝✝

Most think Juan was poisoned by his own brother, Cesare.

✝✝✝

However, unable to resist temptations of the flesh, he soon forgot his vow and filled the Vatican with whores once more. He also "lent" Vatican money to his family, enabling them to buy large estates and to become ever more deeply immersed in Roman

crime. Alexander was turning the papacy into a family business, and the Borgias were using the Holy See as a personal bank.

One evening, Alexander and Cesare attended a supper hosted for them by a cardinal. Both of them accidentally ingested a large amount of poison that was reputedly meant for their host. (Some say that Alexander himself had planted it in the food but had mistakenly eaten the wrong portion.) The pope died, but his son survived.

✝ ✝ ✝

Vatican records piously state that the Holy Father died of a fever that was raging in Rome at the time, but this was certainly not the case.

✝ ✝ ✝

Leaving the Church badly divided and mired in filth and controversy, Alexander was succeeded by a sickly, compromise stopgap pope, Pius III. This ailing pontiff, suffering badly from gout, lasted only seventeen days in office and achieved nothing—while the scandals and sleaze of the Roman Church continued to rage around him unabated.

Leo X (March 17, 1513–December 1, 1521)
Living it up, Medici style

Giovanni de Medici, the son of Lorenzo the Magnificent, really lived it up in style: the floors of several of his palaces were inlaid with gold, his banquets were the talk of Rome, and he kept a private circus for his own pleasure.

Giovanni had been made a priest at the age of seven and was named cardinal-deacon of Santa Maria in Dominica at thirteen. At thirty-seven, he was elected pope, taking the name Leo X, and was virtual ruler of Florence, the Medici power base. He was elevated to the papacy because a number of cardinals wanted a change from his predecessor, the soldier-pope Julius II, who had been preoccupied with worldly matters. From the outset, Leo behaved much like a Renaissance prince. Although he certainly was not a big political or military figure in the style of Julius II, he was not very spiritual either. He loved books, fine wines, extravagant food, art, music, theater, and spectacle.

His pontificate seems to have centered on two things—making Rome the cultural center of Europe and protecting his beloved Florence from foreign domination. In order to safeguard the city, Leo entered into a highly unpopular treaty with

the French, who had scored a number of notable military victories in Italy. They had taken the important center of Milan and looked to be ready to march on Florence; in order to spare the city, Leo surrendered Parma and Piacenza. In return, Florence remained untouched, independent, and still under Medici control. He also granted the French crown the right of nomination to the higher offices of the Church (abbots, priors, and bishops) and the greater part of all benefices within the surrendered area. This served to alienate both the Church and the Italian people.

As far as the increasing power of Protestantism was concerned, Leo did very little. His predecessor Julius had convened several councils—including the Fifth Lateran in 1512—to examine this growing danger as well as other Church concerns. Leo was reluctantly forced to continue them. However, he soon wound most of them up, as they got in the way of his hedonistic lifestyle. His indifference allowed the Protestant Reformation to gather impetus and take hold in many parts of Europe.

As a result of Leo's extravagance, the papacy was now in serious debt, and the pope was forced to pawn or sell off many Vatican treasures to meet his own mounting debts. Worse was to come. The Turkish Empire was rapidly expanding, and the pope was forced by a number of Christian kings to call a crusade

that would limit its power. This entailed the Vatican putting up a substantial amount of money to finance the call to arms— money it didn't have. In order to raise the required finances, Leo embarked upon what might be called a "bargain sale" of Church offices, including cardinals' hats. In addition to the expense of the crusade, the Vatican was building a new St. Peter's; in order to finance *that*, Leo had borrowed heavily, leaving the Christian Church in the embarrassing position of being deeply in debt to Jewish moneylenders. When the sale of Church offices did not bring in enough money to meet all these bills, Leo resorted to other means. He began to sell indulgences on a grand scale.

✦ Indulgence: a purchased forgiveness for a sin that had not yet been committed. These allowed individuals to sin with impunity and, of course, were contrary to scriptural teaching and Church law. ✦

In January 1517, an Augustinian monk named Martin Luther pinned a document detailing ninety-five theses of protest to the door at Wittenberg Cathedral. On receiving a summary of Luther's criticisms in 1518, Leo ordered their suppression and instructed the general of his order to keep him quiet. He would later publish a papal bull, *Decet Romanum Pontificem*, condemning the monk on forty-one counts of heresy and false preaching.

✝✝✝

In a strange twist, Leo praised the future English King Henry VIII as a staunch defender of Catholicism, bestowing on him the title "Defender of the Faith" for his forthright rebuttal of Martin Luther's arguments. Later, during the papacy of Clement VII, Henry would break away from the Catholic Church to found his own Anglican faith.

✝✝✝

Seemingly unperturbed by the growing clamor against the Holy See, Leo continued his extravagant lifestyle, dismissing Protestantism as a passing fancy. He largely ignored the growing spiritual crisis in the Church, instead busying himself with hunting, lavish banquets, and developing Rome into a cultural and hedonistic center. As the religious storm broke around him, Leo suddenly died in 1521 from a bout of malaria, leaving Italy in political turmoil and all the problems of the Church to his successor, the Dutchman Hadrian (Adrian) VI.

GAY POPE
Julius III (February 8, 1550–March 23, 1555)

Although the Church has long considered homosexuality a sin
and a "deep offense against God," this has not stopped men with
homosexual tendencies from assuming the highest office. Much
of their activity has come down to us in hints, whispers, and
innuendo. Pope Paul II (1464–1471), for instance, was widely
rumored to enjoy seeing naked male heretics stretched on a
rack—so much so that he committed "a wicked act" (i.e., masturbation) each time he was in their presence. Meanwhile, Clement
VII (1378–1394) surrounded himself with young pageboys in
tunics cut off above their buttocks, allowing the pope to fondle
them from behind from time to time. Most pontiffs, however,
tried to keep their homosexual leanings a secret while in office—
except for Julius III, who did the opposite, openly flaunting his
sexual preferences and desires when the opportunity arose.

Born Giovanni Maria de Ciocchi del Monte, Julius had
come to prominence during the reign of Pope Julius II, who
himself was described as a sodomite covered with shameful
ulcers. Indeed, it was thought that Julius had been one of the
old pope's lovers as a very young boy. For this, he was rewarded
with the position of assistant chamberlain, a post that may

have been created for him. Following the death of Paul III, Ciocchi del Monte was elected as a compromise candidate and crowned on February 22, 1550.

In 1548, two years before his election to the papacy, he had been walking in the streets of Parma when he saw a young boy being attacked by a trained ape. He managed to save the boy, named Innocenzo, and promptly fell in love with him and brought him home. Various accounts are given as to the boy's age—some say he was fifteen, others seventeen—but there is no doubt that the future pope was seriously taken with him. This infatuation became even stronger when Ciocchi del Monte was elevated to the Holy See. The pontiff urged his brother to adopt the boy, under pain of excommunication, so that Innocenzo might have his own family name. This enabled Julius to bestow upon him the rank of cardinal-nephew.

✝✝✝

The lucrative title of cardinal-nephew was created by the Renaissance popes for members of their own families, to ensure that their illegitimate offspring were provided for.

✝✝✝

This was only one of the positions that the love-struck pope heaped upon the boy—he also made him a cardinal-provost

of Rome and, later, a cardinal, despite objections from certain quarters of the Church. In this role, and acting as a papal secretary, he often visited the pope in his bedchamber "on matters of State" and, according to the Venetian ambassador, also shared his bed. The pope lavished such wealth on Innocenzo that the young beggar boy from Parma became one of the wealthiest men in Italy—wealthier even than the Medicis of Florence.

Innocenzo may have been his favorite, but the pope filled his court with young men—pages, secretaries, and so forth—with

⚔ KEEPER OF THE POPE'S MONKEY ⚔

By far the most attention-grabbing post bestowed on the pope's favorite sidekick was "Keeper of the Pope's Monkey." Despite the attack he'd suffered, Innocenzo reputedly had a special affinity for animals—particularly apes. The title of this paid post allowed much ribald and salacious comment to circulate, and scurrilous satirical pieces were performed throughout Rome, referring to Innocenzo as Julius's "Ganymede"—the youth in Greek fable who submitted to Zeus and became the mythological icon of the catamite. If Julius was aware of this backlash, he gave no sign. Innocenzo used his "special relationship" with the pope to advance his own causes and those of his friends. Those who disliked him branded him "the Cardinal Monkey" and waited for his downfall.

whom he also took his pleasure when it suited him. For example, during a break in an important meeting relating to the Counter-Reformation, a Florentine representative is alleged to have found the pope, dressed in full pontifical robes, sodomizing a young pageboy behind a screen. When confronted on a similar matter, Julius replied that he had granted himself absolution, even from the heinous sin of sodomy. His court seemed to be awash with homosexuality—this was also the period in which Giovanni della Casa, Bishop of Beneventum, wrote his famous 1552 verse-book *De Laudibus Sodomae* (*In Praise of Sodomy*). He dedicated it to Julius III, who received it gratefully and granted it his own personal imprimatur.

Naturally, the pope's behavior was gleefully seized upon by Protestant reformers, who used it to condemn the "evils of the papacy" and the Catholic Church in general. Julius's legacy would continue for several hundred years after his reign and the pope's name became a byword for extreme sexual behavior. This was a time, of course, when the Church was still considering a counter to the Protestant Reformation: what it needed more than anything else was a strong pontiff to guide it—but Julius was no such figure.

Julius's appetite extended beyond the company of young boys. Like the other Renaissance popes, he behaved very much like a hedonistic prince, enjoying good food and fine wines, hosting extravagant banquets, visiting the theater, hunting, and indulging the interests of his own family.

His indifference at this crucial time gave the Reformation an opportunity to take root in Europe, resulting in widespread condemnation of the Vatican even from within the Catholic Church itself. Had the Church not been in crisis, Julius's hedonism might have been allowed to continue.

When French forces and some of the German military revolted against the Holy Roman Emperor, Julius simply retired to a sumptuous new villa he'd built for himself at the Porto del Popolo. He brought along a number of young men, of course, and indulged himself in idle pursuits and sexual excesses, interrupted only by the occasional venture into sacred business. He was frequently visited by Innocenzo, who remained his lover and continued to enjoy papal favor and protection until Julius died of gout in March 1555. Almost at once, the tide turned against the "cardinal-monkey;" he continued living lavishly, but in 1560, he was accused of murder

and rape and imprisoned several times until he died in 1577 at age forty-six.

Julius's legacy was a church mired in sleaze, badly divided, and battered by emerging Protestantism. His successor, Marcellus II, was elected on a reforming ticket and promised to take a grip on the situation. Unfortunately, he died from a sudden stroke before he could achieve anything.

INCOMPETENT POPE
Gregory XIV (December 5, 1590–October 16, 1591)

✝ ✝ ✝

"Stupidity is also a gift of God, but one mustn't misuse it."
—John Paul II

✝ ✝ ✝

The pontificate of Gregory XIV stands out in papal history as one of the most unpopular and least successful. Niccolò Sfondrati, cardinal-priest of Santa Cecilia, was elected by a faction-ridden, acrimonious conclave that had lasted more than two months. Indeed, if it had not been for the support of several pro-Spanish cardinals, he would not have been elected at all. He was reputedly the last in a list of seven contenders and had been largely rejected because of his lack of curial experience. However, the fierce infighting of the conclave pushed him to the fore, and he suddenly found himself pope.

Although elected at the comparatively sprightly age of fifty-five, Gregory was often not in good health and was troubled with pains. He was also something of a hypochondriac and had an almost paranoid distrust of those around him.

Because of his weak state and personal insecurities, the Curia

allowed him to appoint his twenty-nine-year-old nephew, Paolo Emilio Sfondrati, as his cardinal-secretary of state, with wide-ranging powers second only to the pontiff himself. Paolo, however, was completely corrupt and more interested in lining his own pockets than running the Holy See in a proper fashion. Food shortages had left public morale very low, and the Roman people looked to the Church for salvation and solace. What they got instead was exploitation and corruption. There is little doubt that Paolo was involved in "black-market racketeering" and was profiting out of the dire situation in the city. This was done, in many people's eyes, with the tacit approval of his uncle, the pope.

Politically, Gregory abandoned all the conciliatory work of his predecessor Sixtus V, who had worked to mediate in the rivalry between France and Spain. He strongly favored Spain, who had supported his candidacy for the papacy. This only served to antagonize the French cardinals within the Curia. He also took a hard-line position against Protestant French King Henry IV—a popular figure in his own country—and this rallied moderate Catholics to the monarch's cause against the pope.

✝ ✝ ✝

Ironically, King Henry IV later converted to Catholicism.

✝ ✝ ✝

Hostilities between the countries grew as a result of the pope's intervention. When the threat of war loomed, Gregory washed his hands of the issue and retired to his bed, overcome by exhaustion.

As Protestantism gained power, the pope distracted himself with minor infringements rather than establish a logical and tolerant orthodoxy. He called for strict requirements for candidates to the hierarchy; he forbade Mass to be held in private houses; and he prohibited gambling on papal elections. All these measures only served to alienate the public against the papacy. In the face of both public and political discontent, Gregory took to his bed once more, claiming ill health, and left the running of the papacy largely to his corrupt nephew. The crisis deepened: there were riots on the Roman streets, the Curia threatened to revolt, and more and more Catholics began to turn from the Catholic Church toward a Protestant doctrine. Paolo's handling grew increasingly inept, and Gregory withdrew even further from the affairs of the Vatican.

In the end, he simply gave up and died as the winter of 1591 approached, leaving a seemingly insoluble mess for his successor, Innocent IX, who was to reign for only two months.

BLIND POPE

Clement XII (July 12, 1730–February 6, 1740)

In the mid-eighteenth century, the Church found itself in crisis-mode once again. Despite the best efforts of the Council of Trent, Protestantism had taken a firm hold in Western Europe. Many former believers were starting to turn away from Christianity altogether toward forms of humanism and atheism. The thinkers of the Enlightenment often viewed Church practices as "superstitious nonsense" belonging to the Middle Ages, and even many Catholics were ignoring the dictates and edicts of the Church. What was desperately needed was a strong and competent pontiff who would face the challenges of an increasingly secular century. Unfortunately, Clement XII was almost the exact opposite.

Elected at the age of seventy-eight, plagued with gout, and in frail health generally, Clement XII (née Lorenzo Corsini) spent most of his time bedridden and, in the second year of his pontificate, became stone-blind. As his reign wore on, he grew increasingly confused and was forced to rely on others to form and implement his dictates. This allowed room for "personal interpretation" and often corruption, especially by Clement's cardinal-nephew Neri Corsini who virtually ran the Vatican for his own profit.

Faced with such a weak and ineffectual figure at the helm, many Catholic powers in Europe began to ignore the papacy. The Emperor Charles VI declared his own sovereignty over Parma and Piacenza, which up until then had been traditional papal fiefs. The papal lands were overrun by Spanish armies that recruited troops from Rome and tried to raise a revolt among the Roman people. In 1736, Spain and Naples broke off all diplomatic ties with the Holy See. To restore them, Clement had to officially recognize Don Carlos of Spain as king of the Two Sicilies (the territories of Naples and Sicily). This was a humiliating climb-down for a pope who had initially opposed excessive Spanish involvement in Italy.

Nevertheless, the blind pope did beautify Rome, building a new façade on the basilica of St. John Lateran and the magnificent Andrea Corsini Chapel inside the basilica. But perhaps his most enduring landmark is the Piazza di Trevi and the famous Trevi Fountain, which is one of Rome's most famous tourist attractions today.

Sadly, however, Clement is best remembered as the frail, sickly, and elderly pope. Blindness and illness defined his pontificate and compromised the functioning and reputation of the Church at a time when it was already vulnerable. In the

end, the pope could barely rise from his bed; he left meetings with visiting dignitaries to Neri Corsini, who exploited them for his own ends and ensured that even more money went into the Corsini coffers. In fact, the blind man was being robbed by his own family.

✄ THE CORSINIS GET RICH ✄

Neri Corsini used his position as the pope's right-hand man to line his own pockets. He had revived the papal lotteries to raise revenue for the Papal States, and while some did indeed go into public works, a lot of it found its way into the hands of the Corsini family. He also placed new taxes on imports and exports, most of which made him unpopular with Roman merchants. Despite all these measures, the money did not seem to resolve the Vatican's debts, which, Corsini argued, were in fact bigger than anyone had anticipated. These debts were still mounting by the time Clement died in 1740.

"LAST POPE"
Pius VI (February 22, 1775–August 29, 1799)

Pius VI was one of two pontiffs to suffer imprisonment at the hands of the French Emperor, Napoleon Bonaparte (the other being his successor Pius VII). He also enjoyed the fourth longest pontificate in history—behind Pius IX, John Paul II, and Leo XIII—though it was largely regressive and unproductive as far as the Church was concerned. In his defense, it has to be said that the early years of his papacy were marked by various political setbacks, and his later years were spent in captivity in France, where he died in prison at Valence.

Pius's politics were ambiguous—for example, he was perceived as pro-Jesuit by the Jesuits and anti-Jesuit by the anti-Jesuits—and perhaps this aided his election. Lacking any special or charismatic qualities, he was not an intellectual, nor had he any great gift for diplomacy. Indeed, he was so nondescript that the Kingdom of Naples refused to recognize his authority and claimed a right for its monarchs to elect their own bishops. Even the Holy Roman Emperor Joseph II, embracing a spirit of Febronianism (which moved the Church's emphasis away from the papacy and into the episcopate), granted full tolerance for all religions and limited papal intervention to spiritual matters

concerning the Catholic Church. ✦ Febronianism: an eighteenth century view prevalent among some thinkers of the German Church that took its name from Justinius Febronia (John Niklaus von Hontheim). Its beliefs centered on the nationalization of the Catholic Church and the transfer of power from the pope to the individual believer and from the Church to the State. It was directed toward the nationalizing of Catholicism, the restriction of papal power in favor of the episcopacy and the reunion of the Catholic Christian Church in the face of Protestantism. ✦ Since Joseph controlled a large section of Central and Eastern Europe, including Hungary, Germany, Bohemia, and Austria, it was a rather serious matter for the papacy. Pius traveled to Vienna in 1782 (the first pope to leave Rome since 1533) to plead with the Emperor to reverse his decision. He proved such an ineffective negotiator that Joseph, with great courtesy, told him to go back to Rome.

Now Pius decided to take an anti-Jesuit stance in order to please the French Bourbon monarchs and ingratiate himself with France. He tried to put pressure on Frederick II of Prussia and Catherine II of Russia, neither of whom were Roman Catholics and both of whom had allowed Jesuit Societies to flourish within their respective countries. Here, too, he was completely

unsuccessful. In 1780, Catherine had established a novitiate for Jesuits within Russia, while Frederick completely ignored him. It has been suggested, however, that Pius secretly supported the Jesuits and was playing a crafty double game in order to fool the French—but there is no real evidence for this.

In many respects, Pius's reign turned the papacy backward. The Enlightenment had taken hold, and Europe was in intellectual and revolutionary foment. The Church needed a leader who could meet the vast array of new challenges. Pius did not have the intellectual capacity to be such a leader. Instead, he revived old protocols and outdated procedures. He revived papal

✂ WE DON'T NEED THE POPE ✂

The Emperor's position encouraged others to   out the papacy, too—German archbishops for example, decided that they would now run their own church and instructed the pope not to interfere. The 1786 Synod of Pistoia adopted the Four Gallican Articles for the Tuscan Church—the Articles, which originated in France in 1682, had declared the French Church more or less independent of Rome and its bishops exempt from papal authority. Pius officially condemned eighty-five of the Synod's propositions, but he waited until August 1794 to do so and few paid attention.

nepotism, handing out positions to members of his own family and building the Palazzo Braschi for his nephew. Against much advice, he also began a major drainage scheme on the almost impenetrable Pontine Marshes; it proved totally unsuccessful and—with the exorbitant costs of unscrupulous engineers— almost bankrupted the Vatican treasury.

The most significant event during Pius's reign, however, was the French Revolution of 1789. At first, the pope said nothing officially, although he is said to have personally regarded it as a rebellion against a divinely sanctioned social structure, a conspiracy against the Church, and technically a sin. Matters became more serious when on July 12, 1790 the Civil Congregation of the Clergy began to restructure the French Church, making clerics employees of the state and subject to state rather than papal law. They were all forced to swear an oath of loyalty to the French administration. Again, Pius said and did nothing at this time.

In the following year, however, he came out strongly against the new French Republic, denouncing the oath of loyalty, the civil administration, and Thomas Paine's "The Rights of Man," which had been published in 1791 and defended the Revolution as "an offense against God." Pius suspended all clerics who

had taken the civil oath, but stopped short of excommunicating them. All contact between the Holy See and the Revolutionary Council was immediately broken off, and the Council annexed the papal lands of Avignon and Venaissin, where there had been rebellions against the papacy.

The French Church was badly split between those who supported the Revolution and those who remained loyal to Pius. Now was the time for a decisive pope to capitalize on his support and roundly attack the Revolutionary leaders. Pius did nothing but half-heartedly support a pro-monarchist group calling itself the First Coalition, which opposed the new French regime and welcomed a number of pro-Royalists to Rome. However, these were only perceived as token gestures.

In the spring of 1796, Napoleon Bonaparte occupied Milan and demanded that the pope withdraw his condemnation of the Revolution and the Civil Constitution. When Pius petulantly refused, the French invaded the Papal States and defeated the pope's forces. Pius immediately sued for peace. The Peace of Tolentino in 1797 was personally humiliating for Pius and expensive for the Church. The papacy had to pay a huge indemnity as well as hand over valuable manuscripts and paintings.

He also had to hand over large swathes of land in Ferrara, Bologna, and Romagna, which all became Republican territories. In return, the French withdrew for a while and did not pose a threat. An uneasy peace developed, with one side warily watching the other and Bonaparte publicly stating that Pius VI would be "the last pope." After him, the Corsican general promised, the papacy would be dissolved and Italy itself would become a republic. A number of Italians supported that idea and in 1802, the Italian northern states formed a short-lived minor republic as a vassal state to Napoleon's First French Republic. This would collapse in 1805.

The Peace of Tolentino was not to last. There were riots in Rome in support of Revolutionary principles, and a French general was killed. Back in Paris, the senior administration ordered a reinvasion of the Papal States. On February 15, 1798, General Louis Berthier entered Rome, declaring the city a Roman Republic and Pius VI, as head of state, deposed. Pius fled to Florence, where he remained cut off from the machinery of the papacy for sev-

eral months. However, he was soon "taken into custody" by the French Directorate. Concerned that supporting troops would try to rescue him, they brought the pope to Turin and then over the Alps and into Briançon, France, on April 30. From there, he was moved to Valence, where he was held prisoner.

Pius VI died in Valence at the age of eighty-one on August 29, 1799, still a prisoner of the French. He was buried in a local cemetery in an insignificant grave, which nevertheless bore the inscription: "The body of Pius VI, supreme pontiff. Pray for him." Although he was widely disliked, there was genuine grief at his passing, and funerals were held for him in countries not directly controlled by the French Directorate. In 1802, his remains were transferred to St. Peter's in Rome but later moved to the basilica crypt.

Many people, including Napoleon, had predicted that Pius VI would be "the last pope" and that after him the papacy would flounder. However, with unexpected foresight, Pius had left careful instructions for a conclave to elect a successor under emergency conditions. That successor, Luigi Baraba Chiaramonti (Pius VII), would also suffer at the hands of the French. From 1809 to 1814, he was held prisoner in Savona guarded by almost 1,400 French soldiers. This was indeed a very dark time for the papacy, and yet somehow it endured. Despite dire predictions from every quarter, Pius VI was by no means "the last pope."

POOL-PLAYING POPE

Pius IX (June 16, 1846–February 7, 1878)

The pontificate of Pius IX remains the longest in Vatican history at thirty-one years and slightly over seven months. Pius oversaw the early stirrings of what might be called the modern papacy; in fact, the pope himself was so modern that he was just as comfortable sinking the eight ball as he was saying the rosary.

Unlike many of his predecessors, Giovanni Maria Mastai-Ferretti's origins in the Vatican were humble. Although his father was a count who could have secured him religious office, he began his career as a soldier in the papal guard. While serving, he developed a keen interest in both billiards and pool and was by all accounts an extremely able and skilled player.

Given his wealthy background, it was rather unlikely that he would stay a soldier for long; he was ordained into the priesthood in 1819, despite a problem with epilepsy, and named archbishop of Spoleto in 1827. Upon the death of Gregory XVI (1831–1846), the cardinals were badly split between Cardinal Luigi Lambruschini, the former papal secretary of state, and the more liberal Cardinal Tomasso Gizzi, a former apostolic nuncio to Switzerland. ✦ Nuncio: from the Latin word "numtius," meaning "envoy;" a representative of the pope or head of a

diplomatic mission from the Holy See. ✦ The deadlock between the two men was unbreakable, so as a sort of compromise the fifty-four-year-old Cardinal Mastai-Ferretti suddenly found himself elected as pope. It was not a position he particularly wanted, but he accepted it anyway, taking the name Pius IX. When the white smoke emerged, signaling the election of a new pontiff, many thought that Cardinal Gizzi had become pope. After the austere and dogmatic reign of Gregory XVI, many longed for a more liberal period and greeted the assumption with delight. In Cardinal Gizzi's hometown of Ceccano, there was much rejoicing and parading through the streets. The revelation that the new pope was *not* Cardinal Gizzi, but Cardinal Mastai, was greeted with only lukewarm applause. He was not a popular choice. Nevertheless, he had the good sense to make Cardinal Gizzi his secretary of state, and all of liberal Europe welcomed the move. Pius went on to become one of the great reforming popes, and his reign was one of the most important throughout the nineteenth century, helping define the papacy for decades to come.

✝ ✝ ✝

Pius IX tried to restore the Vatican to old and established ways. For example, the First Vatican Council was to reaffirm traditional values and the sovereignty of the pontiff in all

areas of life—but actually laid the foundations for a new and vibrant papacy.

✝✝✝

However, the pontiff had a secret. Pius's love of billiards and pool had never left him; indeed, it had turned into something of an obsession. Upon election to the papacy, he promptly installed two billiard tables—one in his retreat at Castel Gandolfo and one in the Vatican itself. He was a skilled and cunning player, insisting that many of his cardinals learn how to play pool so that he could play against them; he invariably won. He also played regularly against members of the Vatican Guard. Apparently, the pope even played for money, which would certainly be a sin in papal terms!

✝✝✝

Some have said that in terms of both style and temperament, Pius IX would not have looked out of place in the pool halls of the South Bronx in New York—now there's an image to contend with!

✝✝✝

Despite his successful reforms and obviously fun-loving side, Pius IX remained a deeply unpopular pope with everyone but the Roman working classes.

NAZI POPE

Pius XII (March 2, 1939–October 9, 1958)

The pontificate of Pius XII has always had a tinge of controversy surrounding it, largely because of the pope's previous activities as Cardinal Eugenio Pacelli, cardinal secretary of state in relation to Nazi Germany. Indeed, the relationship between the pontiff and Adolph Hitler's Third Reich has been the subject of much recent debate, with many books and television documentaries analyzing the issue.

After a one-day conclave, Eugenio Pacelli was elected pope on March 2, 1939, just as the Second World War was about to erupt. His diplomatic skills, it was suggested, were just what the Vatican needed in those turbulent times, and he had been a papal nuncio to Germany with a great understanding of German culture. If anyone could avert war and the rise of Nazism, it should have been he. However, some detractors point to the then-cardinal's 1933 signing of the *Reichskonkordat*, which limited Church intervention in political matters within Germany and gave the support of the clergy to the German administration. According to Pacelli, it was intended to safeguard the position of Catholics in Bavaria, a staunchly Catholic area of Germany; but some say it was used to covertly support the Nazis in order to

prevent the spread of Communism, with which the Church was more concerned. Critics allege that Pacelli used the treaty to stop his predecessor, Pius XI, from speaking out against *Kristallnacht* (the Night of Broken Glass) in 1938, when Nazi sympathizers attacked synagogues, Jewish houses, and businesses in several major German cities.

Pacelli has also been criticized for the closeness of his relationship with the right-wing Ludwig Kaas, a German politician (chairman of the Centre Party) and Catholic priest. Kaas, it is argued, had strong links to the Nazis, supporting them to slow the Communist advance in Germany. Pacelli reputedly viewed Communism as a much greater evil than Nazism and was personally prepared to support Hitler and the Nazi Movement. This seemed to be confirmed by two separate papal statements issued by Pius XII (1944 and 1946), in which he implicitly exonerated Germany from any notion of collective guilt.

Pius had also been criticized by historians for his failure to speak out against the persecution of Jews. His predecessor, Pius XI, had officially condemned the racism espoused by Italian Fascists in the encyclical *Non abbiamo bisogno* ("We have no need"), even though he had openly supported the Spanish dictator Generalissimo Francisco Franco during the Spanish Civil

War (1936–1939). Pius XII, however, remained "neutral" in regard to the rise of the Nazi Party, leading to the allegation in some quarters that he was "Hitler's pope." But while he did not approve of the Allies' demand for unconditional German surrender at Casablanca in 1943, he *also* did not approve of Hitler's attack on Russia. Still, he didn't make a single gesture of protest against the Nazi outrages.

In all fairness, the pope *did* denounce the extermination of peoples based on race, albeit couched in terms so general as to be ineffective. Furthermore, when Hitler occupied Rome on September 10, 1943, the Vatican State became a sanctuary for the city's refugees, including Jews, who came under the express protection of the pope.

Nevertheless, the pope's seeming indifference to the Holocaust tainted his papacy and strengthened his reputation as a covert Nazi sympathizer. Perhaps such a perception is an unfair one. Pius XII was by nature a conservative who valued the primacy of the Catholic Church in a rapidly changing world. He saw the Church as an independent spiritual entity that, while protecting the souls of the poor and downtrodden, must remain outside politics to be wholly effective. While there is no doubt that he could have done much more to distance himself from

Nazism and its attendant horrors, perhaps the charge that he was "Hitler's pope" is unwarranted.

Always a firm believer in the truth of Catholic doctrine, Pius XII did little to build bridges with the Protestant faith or to initiate any form of ecumenical dialogue. Nevertheless, when he died at Castel Gandolfo in 1958, he had achieved considerable credibility and influence for the Catholic Church, even among non-Catholics. In many respects, he had laid the foundations for the modern papacy, and the work of ecumenism would fall to his successor, the energetic John XXIII.

PASTA-LOVING POPE

John XXIII (October 28, 1958–June 3, 1963)

"It often happens that I wake up at night and begin to think about a serious problem and decide I must tell the pope about it. Then I wake up completely and remember that I am the pope."

—John XXIII

In their daily lives, popes are expected to be austere and to show a holy restraint toward worldly things. This usually means that they dine in moderation, eschewing the worldly pleasures of the laden table. (Of course, this has not always been the case. The popes of the Renaissance, for example, certainly enjoyed their food.) In the sobering times of the mid–twentieth century, people looked to the papacy as a model of restraint. However, this could not be said of Angelo Roncalli, who was to become Pope John XXIII, one of the most beloved pontiffs in the history of the Holy See.

When elected, his choice of papal name outraged traditionalists. He insisted on taking John XXIII, even though the previous pontiff to hold that name had been an antipope during the Great Western Schism (see "Struck-Off Popes: John XXIII," page 114) and had brought the papacy into disrepute. For many who still believed in the supremacy of the Catholic Church, the prospect of his reign spelled disaster. And the conservative churchmen

who had flourished under Pius XII were right to be apprehensive, for the new pontiff began reaching out to the laity and building bridges with the Protestants. John XXIII set about reforming the Church through the Second Vatican Council, or Vatican II, as it became known.

✝ ✝ ✝

Vatican II, founded in October 1962, was an ecumenical council designed to make the Church more accessible and develop links with Protestantism.

✝ ✝ ✝

No pope in the history of Christendom was as committed to Christian unity as John XXIII; but, inevitably, such a position made him deeply unpopular among conservatives and traditionalists within the Catholic Church.

But in spite of his dissenters, he was an extremely popular pope, feted everywhere he went and completely disarming those in the wider world who might have been opposed to him. When he died in 1963, the Union Jack flew at half-mast as a sign of respect, even in the pro-Unionist, anti-Catholic city of Belfast. This was seen as a measure of his universal popularity throughout the world.

John was so popular that it was suggested he be made a saint when he died. This alarmed many conservatives, who thought

the pontiff had done incredible harm to Church ideals. They were determined to deny him sainthood, but they needed an excuse—and they found it in the former pope's one weakness.

True to his Italian heritage, John XXIII loved food, particularly pasta. He couldn't seem to get enough of it. Late at night— John famously needed very little sleep—he would prowl around the Vatican kitchens, raiding the fridges as he went. In the early hours of the morning, he was sometimes found devouring huge platefuls of spaghetti and tomato sauce—in full pontifical robes. The pasta habit allowed detractors to claim that the pope was not as saintly as he appeared because "the Holy Father had given in to the awful sin of gluttony;" and this, apparently, was enough to debar him from formal sainthood. His late-night pasta feasts came at a high price.

⚜ COOKING WITH THE POPE ⚜

Although he certainly enjoyed his food, John XXIII was not as big a glutton as Pius V (1566–1572), who absolutely adored what he ate and who was, apparently, an excellent cook. Indeed, his most widely sought-after work was not a religious treatise nor a papal encyclical, but a cookbook, *The Cooking Secrets of Pope Pius V*, which was something of a bestseller in its day. Unlike John, however, Pius's gluttony did not stand in the way of his sainthood.

SUED POPE
Paul VI (June 21, 1963–August 6, 1978)

Given that the Vatican is estimated to be worth at least one billion dollars, Mr. William Sheffield's action against the pope for the sum of $428.50 may seem insignificant. But, in the entire history of the papacy, he was the only person to ever successfully sue a pope in a court of law.

The California law student had paid a deposit of sixty dollars to secure a puppy for himself at a Swiss monastery; but the pup was never delivered, and the deposit was not returned. Sheffield claimed that Paul IV, as head of the Church, was responsible for the goings on at the monastery; and so he began proceedings against the Vicar of Christ in order to resolve the puppy debacle.

In considering the case, an Alameda County superior judge found that the pope was similar to a managing director of a firm. His firm had agreed to provide the animal and was therefore liable for its business obligations. Consequently, he ruled in favor of Sheffield for the full value of the dog plus legal costs. Sheffield hasn't had any luck enforcing the judgment or collecting the money. Nor has the Vatican ever acknowledged the order made against it.

TOP OF THE POPES
John Paul II (October 16, 1978–April 2, 2005)

Nowadays, recording stars are thought of as rockers or rap artists. But the *pope?* It may seem strange, but it's true. As the first Slavic pope in history, Karol Wojtyla (John Paul II) reflected the many facets of his Eastern-European home: he was a keen sportsman, an extremely able poet, and a reasonably good singer.

John Paul II took a keen interest in many sports, particularly skiing and soccer. At his consecration, John Paul dispensed with tradition and demanded that the sacred ceremony be held several hours early, so he could be back at the Vatican in time to put his feet up and watch an important soccer game on television.

✝ ✝ ✝

It seemed natural, then, that such a media-friendly pontiff should venture into the world of CDs and MP3s. John Paul II's recording career began in 1995 with a Spanish album called *Pope of the Rosary.* Released on the Prism label, the record of inspirational religious material was designed to build on the pontiff's successful tour of Spain in July 1994; it was an instant hit among the Spanish faithful as well as in South America. Indeed, it was so successful that an Italian/Latin version was released in 1998.

Simply entitled *The Rosary*, the album consisted of devotional and meditation material, part spoken and part sung. This was also a best seller, even outperforming boy bands such as Take That in some areas of Italy. With his CDs classed under the "rock and pop" category in music stores, the pope was becoming a pop star—and a bigger celebrity than many rockers and rap artists in certain regions of Europe.

In 1999, the pope released his biggest album, *Abba Pater*, on the mainstream Sony label. Its release was accompanied by an array of papal merchandise, including posters of the pope with Mother Teresa of Calcutta. In terms of sales, this was his most successful album, outselling a number of the label's other acts. He followed it up in 2000 with the album *Papal Blessing* on Gateway Records.

As with many artists, interest in Pope John Paul's work increased after he died. And record companies capitalized on the pontiff's passing: PID released *Poems of Karol Wojtyla*, accompanied by a DVD, and then followed it with the 2006 *Pilgrim of Peace*. A further album of previously unheard devotional material, *Cantos de la Misa Del Papa* (*Chants from the Pope's Mass*), was released at the end of 2007. In many respects, John Paul II had become as big a recording legend as Elvis, and in a recording sense, he is truly "Top of the Popes."

MISNUMBERED POPE
Benedict XVI (April 19, 2005–)

The current pope, Benedict XVI, may only be Benedict XV. Moreover, he may well have committed heresy by taking the wrong number—and several of his namesake predecessors may have done likewise. The problem arises during the brief and turbulent "pontificate" of Benedict X (1058–1059).

A series of pontiffs imposed by the German Emperor Henry III had finally come to an end with the death of Pope Victor II in 1057. Powerful Roman families elected a pope of their own, Stephen IX (X), without notifying the Imperial German Court, as they were obliged to under the terms of a treaty. However, Stephen's weak and faltering reign ended merely seven months later in March 1058, but not before he named a successor—an adviser named Hildebrand who was in Germany at that time negotiating peace and reform with the German court.

Fearing that Hildebrand might make too many concessions, an anti-reformist group of Roman families elected a pope in his absence, John, cardinal-bishop of Valletri, who took the name Benedict X. Supported by some of the most powerful families in Rome, the new pope took office on April 5, ignoring his predecessor's wishes as well as those of Hildebrand's supporters,

many of whom were clergy. The Curia subsequently descended into squabbling and feuding, which included allegations of bribery and papal corruption.

When word reached Hildebrand in Germany, he decided that negotiations were at too delicate a stage for him to return; instead, he nominated Gerard, bishop of Florence, as the next pope. Gerard was duly elected, taking the name Nicholas II, and promptly excommunicated Benedict. Backed by armies from sympathetic nobles, Nicholas entered Rome and forced Benedict to flee.

However, Benedict still had some supporters—including Gerard of Galeria—and was able to mount his own army with the intention of retaking Rome. Nicholas's army marched to meet them, and the rivals clashed at Campagna in 1059. Even though the outcome was not as conclusive as Nicholas had hoped, Benedict's support crumbled and he conceded the papacy and denounced himself as a heretic. He further declared that he had never been pope and threw himself on Nicholas's mercy.

In return for this admission, Nicholas allowed Benedict to go free. But when Hildebrand returned from Germany in 1060, he had him arrested as a traitor to the Church. Benedict remained

imprisoned until he died in either 1073 or 1080. He was kept well away from public view, presumably so people would forget about him. When Hildebrand became pope, as Gregory VII in 1073, he declared that Benedict X had never existed and that all reference to him should be excised from Vatican records. Furthermore, he ordered that any acknowledgement of such a pope—whether by the laity or subsequent pontiffs—would be counted as rank heresy punishable by instant excommunication. So, essentially, near the end of the eleventh century, Pope Benedict X disappeared.

More than a century later in 1303, Niccolò Boccasini, cardinal-bishop of Ostia, chose the name Benedict, which had been the baptismal name of his predecessor, Boniface VIII, when he was elected as pope. The Curia pleaded with him to take the number ten, but he insisted on Benedict XI. Technically, this was heresy since it contravened Church doctrine and implied recognition of Benedict X's claim to the papacy. But no action was taken.

✝ ✝ ✝

Even today, Vatican records pass directly from Benedict IX to Benedict XI with no mention of Benedict X.

✝ ✝ ✝

Subsequent Benedicts took their numbering from Benedict XI, thus tacitly acknowledging the antipope and risking excommunication. Benedict XII, a French pope elected in Avignon, reigned from 1335 to 1342. There were then two popes named Benedict XIII: the first, another Avignon pontiff, reigned from 1394 to 1407 during the Great Western Schism; the second reigned from 1724 to 1730. Pietro Francesco Orsini actually denounced the Avignon pope before assuming his name—he had originally considered taking the name Benedict XIV, but realized that this would have legitimized the French pontiff. Then, Benedict XIV reigned from 1740 to 1758, and Benedict XV from 1914 to 1922.

So, by adopting the title Benedict XVI instead of Benedict XV, did current pontiff Joseph Ratzinger commit rank heresy by acknowledging the reign of Benedict X? Should he now formally excommunicate himself? An intriguing question and one perhaps only the Vatican can answer.

CONCLUSION

Perhaps in contrast to the current image of a refined and graceful pope, papal history has often been a turbulent affair, filled with strange, sometimes violent, and certainly colorful characters. The office of pope is unmatched by any other ministry in the world in terms of splendor, authority, and religious mystery—but it has been so poorly understood, often even by those who have occupied it.

Today, the papacy is often perceived in terms of its modern status in the world—embodying a strong centrality of belief as well as power and sanctity. It's viewed as a *constant* in the religious world, something that has always been the way it appears today. But this is not the case.

Throughout history, the papacy has often been viewed as much more than simply a spiritual institution. The pope *ruled* the Church in the same way that an earthly monarch might rule his or her kingdom.

And it should not be forgotten that, no matter how high the spiritual calling, and even though they may have been chosen by God, popes are human, prone to temptation and failure.